RELIGION

AS WE KNOW IT

An Origin Story

JACK MILES

W. W. NORTON & COMPANY
Independent Publishers Since 1923

Portions previously published in *The Norton Anthology of World Religions*, copyright © 2015 by W. W. Norton & Company, Inc.

For information about permission to reproduce selections from this book, write to Permissions, W. W. Norton & Company, Inc., 500 Fifth Avenue, New York, NY 10110

For information about special discounts for bulk purchases, please contact W. W. Norton Special Sales at specialsales@wwnorton.com or 800-233-4830

Manufacturing by Lake Book Manufacturing
Book design by Chris Welch
Production manager: Beth Steidle

Library of Congress Cataloging-in-Publication Data

Names: Miles, Jack, 1942– author.
Title: Religion as we know it : an origin story / Jack Miles.
Description: First edition. | New York : W. W. Norton & Company, Inc., [2020] | Includes bibliographical references and index.
Identifiers: LCCN 2019026444 | ISBN 9781324002789 (paperback) | ISBN 9781324002796 (epub)
Subjects: LCSH: Western countries—Religion. | Christianity—Influence. | Religion—Study and teaching—Western countries—History. | Religion and civilization.
Classification: LCC BL689 .M55 2020 | DDC 200.9—dc23
LC record available at https://lccn.loc.gov/2019026444

W. W. Norton & Company, Inc., 500 Fifth Avenue, New York, N.Y. 10110
www.wwnorton.com

W. W. Norton & Company Ltd., 15 Carlisle Street, London W1D 3BS

1 2 3 4 5 6 7 8 9 0

For KM and her BF

Gods here?
Who can know?
Not I.
Yet I sigh
and tears flow,
tear on tear.

—SAIGYŌ HŌSHI (1118–1190)
ON VISITING THE GRAND SHRINE AT ISE

CONTENTS

PREFACE

The United States of America practices many religions, and *pluralism* in American usage is a term that aims to turn the arguably neutral fact of plural religions into an American value: pluralism. If an American favors pluralism, in other words, then she thinks it good rather than bad that America practices many religions and would regret rather than applaud the replacement of the nation's many religions by some one religion, even her own.

Do Americans in fact favor pluralism? Though many surely do, they do so no doubt to a somewhat varying degree. Nonetheless, nearly ten years ago, when newly appointed as the general editor of the American reference work later to be published as *The Norton Anthology of World Religions,* I chose to assume that American pluralism enjoyed the support of at least a comfortable majority. A majority of Americans, I chose to assume, would welcome a work taking the multiplicity of American religion as not just as a bare fact but also, on balance, as a good thing in our moment of cultural globalization.

I haven't abandoned that assumption. Yet as the decision has now been made to publish my general introduction to the *NAWR* as a separate book, the moment is at hand to reveal how a nagging, complicating background thought both challenged that first assumption in a surprising way and further shaped the work that W. W. Norton & Company eventually published (and that, needless to say, I commend to the readers of this second edition of its introduction).

The Usual Sense of the Word

At the time when Norton approached me about undertaking this work, I had been involved in the study of religion for several decades and had taken part in innumerable public discussions of the subject. What nagged at me was something that had occurred repeatedly in those discussions. Time and again, I had heard someone rise to say that one religion or another "is not a religion in the usual sense of the word" or "not a religion in the mainstream sense of the word." An alternate formulation would sometimes be "_____ is not a religion, it's a way of life." Still another would be, "_____ is not a religion, it's just a part of being _____" and a national identifier would then be supplied. Finally, a frequent formulation would be simply "_____ is not a religion in your sense of the word," with the referent of "your" left quite vague. Whom did the speaker have in mind?

A given speaker might go on to make a perfectly plausible case for why Hopi folk belief and ritual or Shinto or Daoism or some form of Hinduism or even Judaism was misconstrued when taken to be a religion in the usual sense of the word. But who owned that usual sense? Where had it come from? And did it not claim at least enough continuing validity or relevance to bring people of diverse religions together for discussion and debate?

That question did have to be asked, for why assemble people from various religions to talk of any one religion when that religion is then declared not to be a religion in the first place? And what happens to the notion of pluralism if, in fact, there does not exist a plurality of different religions but only a plurality of miscellaneous activities all of which people have for some perverse reason been *calling* religions? And, by the way, who are these presumptuous people? Where and how did they receive or invent their usual sense of the word? And how has their sense of the word acquired such widespread acceptance that speakers still find it necessary to formally dissociate from it? American culture, by the term *pluralism,* has clearly embraced the three-fold notion that there are, yes, many different religions; that they are all somehow comparable to one another; and, crucially, that they are all more or less welcome in the United States. Has this embrace been all along a huge cultural mistake?

Finally, I had to wonder, when speakers dissociated themselves from the term *religion,* did the dissociation actually quite work? It often seemed to me that speakers who repudiated the applicability of the word *religion* to their particular un-religion would later circle back and use the word in spite of themselves in the very sense that they had repudiated. However objectionable, had the word in the usual sense become somehow unavoidable or indispensable?

The phrase "as we know it" in the title of this book refers to religion "as we *talk* about it." The title thus refers to the very sense of the word *religion* that I have just now been discussing. Early in my introduction to *The Norton Anthology of World Religions,* the reader encounters the following deliberately casual and unchallenging sentence:

> What is religion? The word exists in the English language, and people have some commonsense notion of what it refers to. Most understand it as one kind of human activity standing alongside other kinds, such as business, politics, warfare, art, law, sport, or science.

My decision for the organization of *The Norton Anthology of World Religions* was that we would begin with this "commonsense notion" rather than with a theoretically ambitious definition of religion, an academic definition that I would then be required to impose on my six associate editors, each of whom was far more learned than I about one of the six traditions anthologized. My decision was, first, to acknowledge that various competing academic theories of religion do exist and that they define the word quite differently; second, to note that no theory, no definition, has acquired universal acceptance; but then, third and at length, to proceed to give this very commonsense notion, however academically objectionable it might be, as plausible a history as I could manage, stretching back to its very beginning and forward, at the very end, to the American twentieth century. The result was an origin story, the origin story of this book's subtitle.

What makes the everyday American understanding of religion objectionable when extended to cultures very different from the American or European can be traced to the phrase "one kind of human activity alongside other kinds." This ostensibly innocuous phrase has an explosive, disruptive potential because it asserts that religion stands indeed *alongside* the other activities mentioned—in other words, that it is *separable* from and *distin-*

guishable from them. But this is just the assertion that turns out to be objectionable when applied to "religions" (the term immediately comes into question) that are practiced in a way or in a context that makes them indistinguishable and inseparable from business, politics, warfare, law, and so forth down a familiar list of human activities, including even entertainment, not to speak of such larger background realities as language, calendar, marriage, diet, and nationality.

Over the years, those speakers whom I had found most clarifying and instructive, though they may have puzzled me at the time, were those who adopted a stance of disputatious protest against either Christian missionary activity or related Western colonialism and continuing cultural hegemony. Such would be my experience when I would hear an Indian speaker say, "What you people call Hinduism is for me just part of being Indian"; or when I would hear a Jewish speaker say, "Judaism is not a religion, Judaism is a way of life." Hopi religion exists only in the Western Hemisphere, but I once heard a student of that religion say and with good reason, "The Hopi do not have a religion in the Western sense of the word."

Western in that sentence referred not to geography but to culture—namely, to the European culture that started to spread around the world with the great Spanish and Portuguese explorers of the late fifteenth and sixteenth centuries and went on, through later colonialism and the spread of Western ideas of all kinds, to dominate much of the world. This culture, Western culture, has long approached religion in a way profoundly shaped by Christian assumptions, and Christianity had indeed, and very early on, introduced a separation of what it chose to regard as religiously significant from the rest of its adherents' worldly lives. This being the case, the story of how just that artificial separation was made for the first time and then how the habit of making it spread to Europe and outward from Europe—through both missionary activity and secular Western colonialism—becomes the origin story of "religion as we know it." To say that the habit spread is not to say that it was always welcome, but neither is it to deny that it often enough took hold and—its Christian origin quite forgotten—came to be taken for granted. Cultures, after all, do borrow from one another and, over time, assimilate and indigenize what has been borrowed. Western coinages like *Hinduism, Buddhism, Daoism,* and so forth do undeniably squeeze large, complex social and historical realities into the frame of religion "as we know it," but at this late date, thanks to globalization and international migration, the option of simply retiring or retracting such terms scarcely exists. The affected populations themselves now have ownership rights and would exercise them.

This book's origin story is told largely in the long section entitled "How Christian Europe Learned to Compare Religions," just as it originally was told in a section by the same title in the general introduction to *The Norton Anthology of World Religions.* Early in that section, I wrote:

> Through most of world history, in most parts of the world, what we are accustomed to call religion, ethnicity, and culture have been inextricable parts of a single whole. How did Christianity begin to become an exception to this general rule? On the one hand, it appropriated a set of Jewish religious ideas—including monotheism, revelation, covenant, scripture, sin, repentance, forgiveness, salvation, prophecy, messianism, and

apocalypticism—without adopting the rest of the Jewish way of life. On the other hand, it universalized these Jewish religious ideas, creating a new social entity, the church, through which non-Jews could be initiated into an enlarged version of the ancestral Jewish covenant with God.

With hindsight, I would now like to refine or extend this claim in three regards.

First, the Jews who founded Christianity began most clearly to abstract the mentioned set of "religious ideas" from the rest of the Jewish way of life *in the process* of admitting non-Jews to their revised and enlarged sense of the Jewish covenant with God. Jews who became Christian simply by recognizing Jesus as the Jewish Messiah did not at that moment or by that action cease living as Jews. But then, by the same token, Egyptians or Armenians or Macedonians who later embraced a set of dynamic Jewish ideas as part and parcel of accepting Jesus as the Jewish Messiah were not required by that act to become Jews or to cease living in other regards as Egyptians or Armenians or Macedonians. Yet the embrace by so many non-Jews of these originally Jewish ideas almost certainly had the effect over time of severing those ideas not just from the rest of the Jews' way of life but also from the rest of *anyone*'s way of life. To be sure, an almost equally powerful tendency toward reintegration would repeatedly bring about the fusion of Christian identity with the way of life of one nation or another, even one empire or another. Nonetheless a consequential severing took place in principle and could reassert itself at any time.

Second, the act of abstracting Jewish *religious* ideas from the rest of a rich and complex Jewish way of life had the tacit effect of defining the rest of that way of life as somehow *not* religious. For centuries, Jews had distinguished their own true, native worship from the false, alien worship of all others. But now there arose a distinction not just between the Jewish God as the one true or "living" God and other purported gods but also between the religiously consequential or essential parts of the Jewish way of life itself and the rest of that way of life, now taken to be not wrong but only religiously inconsequential or nonessential. This distinction when first made did not amount to a full-fledged distinction between the religious and the secular, but it laid the egg from which that immensely influential later distinction would hatch. Before that point would be reached, Medieval Europe would for centuries incarnate the same key distinction by dividing the personnel of Christendom into the "religious" (monks and nuns) and the "laity" (everyone else: all those engaged in "worldly" pursuits). The Protestant Reformation would challenge this distinction, honoring once worldly pursuits as no less holy in principle than formally religious pursuits and the laity, who engaged in such worldly pursuits, as no less holy in principle than the clergy. The Protestant challenge had, to be sure, lasting consequences. However, the "Great Secularization" of the late seventeenth and the eighteenth centuries would paradoxically revive and embrace the prior distinction while gradually elevating secular pursuits *above* religious ones. Secularization has been a profoundly transformative cultural process, and yet the transformation has necessarily reinforced the originally Christian notion of religion as *separable* from the range of other pursuits whose autonomy secularization has so insisted on.

Third, the early modern study of world religions beyond the West was at first essentially the study of those religions naïvely taken as exotic versions of a reality whose domestic version was Christianity. That is, it was the uncritical study of the non-Christian religions of the world as if they all routinely understood themselves to be, like Christianity, separate domains open for adoption by any sincerely interested party. By this assumption, the religions of South and East Asia and the indigenous religions of Africa and the Americas were misconstrued rather as Christendom had long since misconstrued Judaism, Greco-Roman polytheism, and—to a degree—even Islam. In more recent centuries, more sophisticated students of religion have quite successfully challenged this naïve assumption. Thanks to a substantial academic literature, a more integralist understanding has taken hold which posits that religion, culture, and ethnicity are de facto often found in a fusion so seamless and taken for granted that its practitioners scarcely even have a name for it.

Yet the now solidly established Western assumption that law, politics, art, science, and so forth are inherently autonomous activities, independent of and by all means to be kept separate from the increasingly sequestered realm of religion, has remained influential far beyond the geographical West. Autonomy from religion for all these activities—a derivatively Christian notion whose ancestry is now rarely remembered—has been a crucial element in the rise of *modernity*. And the encounter with modernity has in turn occasioned a crisis in the histories of all six of the major living, international traditions—beginning, of course, with Christianity itself—as these histories are outlined in the table of contents of *The Norton Anthology of World Religions*. In this way, the West, behind it Christianity, and behind Christianity Judaism, has been both a disruptive and a formative force in cultures once untouched by the notion of religion as "we" (of the West) know it. The latest chapters in each of the six large histories anthologized are thus, each in its own way, so many sequels to the origin story.

Now, to say that religion is a separate domain is not, when all is said and done, to say all that much about it. If this notion, now so much a part of American common sense about religion, arose somehow two thousand years ago in the abstraction of a set of dynamic Jewish religious ideas from the rest of the Jewish way of life, how did those Jewish ideas arise in the first place? What was their source? And if other societies—earlier, later, or contemporaneous with Rabbinic Judaism—developed other, different, semireligious or quasi-religious or equivalently religious ideas, did they all spring from the same source? What is the origin story behind all these origin stories, and how far back in human evolution must we go to find it? Was religion an adaptive or maladaptive behavior for prehistoric *Homo sapiens*? Is its taproot individual or social? If social, can it be regarded as a human social analogue to some of the extravagant, sometimes maladaptive but nonetheless durable animal mating rituals described in Richard O. Prum's *The Evolution of Beauty*? Has religion, like the peacock's tail and like art in all its wasteful madness, been a part of how societies survive, thrive, and reproduce themselves over time? Or, if its taproot is individual, then what of mysticism, and what of the anarchic intuition of something beyond all social arrangements that enables their revision or empowers their revolutionary overthrow?

Questions like these can so very easily be multiplied. They are entirely legitimate and even deeply engaging. To ask them, however, is to ask about religion not as we know it but rather as we might now proceed to *study* it. It is to admit that we do not fully understand religion any more than we fully understand such other deep-rooted, universally attested human behaviors as language, art, and play. *The Norton Anthology of World Religions* acknowledges the existence and importance of—but does not adjudicate among—theories of religion that attempt to answer such questions. Instead, the anthology assembles and organizes a large body of texts that students and teachers alike may take as relevant evidence when evaluating competing theories. The goal of the anthology's introduction, now published separately with this new preface, is simply to trace religion "as we know it" to its origin, then to follow the story of its growth and its spread, and, finally, to acknowledge how this powerful but undoubtedly limited way of knowing religions has both enabled their comparison and distorted it down to our own day. The resulting origin story has some of the interest that all origin stories have. It matters most, however, because its darker consequences linger longer the more they are ignored.

Postscript to a Postscript

In the original two-volume hardcover edition of *The Norton Anthology of World Religions* and only in that edition, my general introduction ends— untypically for a reference work—with a section entitled "Concluding Unscholarly Postscript." That title alludes silently to Søren Kierkegaard's 1846 *Concluding Unscientific Postscript* (to his *Philosophical Fragments*), one of his several pseudonymously published essays. Kierkegaard, more influentially than any other modern philosopher, insisted on the legitimacy of subjective, personal experience and subjective truth alongside objective, impersonal knowledge and objective truth.

By and large, reference works aim to synthesize objective, impersonal, generally accepted knowledge of their target subjects. True, by entrusting the six religious traditions anthologized in *The Norton Anthology of World Religions* to six exceptionally accomplished individual scholars rather than to six committees, I had already enabled emphases in each case that would not be shared by all experts in the respective six fields. Subjectivity in that modest form, however, was not the kind of subjectivity that Kierkegaard championed in religion and that many ordinary readers intuitively seek as well.

I acknowledged those readers in the opening paragraphs of my postscript:

As *The Norton Anthology of World Religions* goes to press, I am confident as general editor, having read every word in it at least once over the course of the past nine years, that we have produced a tool that can usefully serve many different purposes, many different agendas. Yet I am aware, too, that when religion is the subject, however academically and dispassionately a scholar may discuss it, readers will ask, "But where are you personally? What is your religion? Are you religious or not?"

These are not scholarly questions, and scholars have every reason to decline them. However, readers also have every reason to ask them and to wonder about the answers when none is forthcoming. The postscript that follows here is a small, personal, and decidedly unscholarly attempt to concede a little something to this legitimate curiosity. The nature of the subject seems to me to constitute an argument for a brief and modest bending of the normal academic rules.

By the "normal academic rules," I meant, in particular, the academic rules that would rule out anything so personal within a collectively authored reference work. Accordingly, I had already asked my six associate editors whether they favored or opposed my adding an extended, subjective, autobiographical meditation to our anthology or not. Five were in favor, one opposed, so W. W. Norton proceeded to include the postscript, but, deferring to the dissenter, I later insisted that it be excluded from the subsequent six-volume paperback edition.

The subjective, autobiographical memoir of my own religiosity that then followed and that is now reissued with a new title as the conclusion of this book reflects above all my decades-long preoccupation with the impact of natural science upon religion. For me, this question has had little or nothing to do with the replacement of an ancient Semitic cosmology with our modern scientific cosmology or with the historicity of the many biblical miracles—the Parting of the Red Sea, the Resurrection of Christ, and so forth. It has been rather a matter of wondering whether and how, as thinkers like Bertrand Russell and Jacques Monod have seemed to think possible or inevitable, science or some ideology directly derived from science could somehow meet the existential needs that religion has historically met. The challenge of living a human life is not the challenge that science sets out to meet, so how are those to proceed who are left with only what science gives them to work with? How do they—how do we if we are they—go about living meaningful lives?

My concern, then, was existential rather than apologetic. My aim was not in the first instance to "rescue" religion but rather to identify for my own private purposes an expedient or range of expedients, which might or might not include religion in some form, that could provide me some degree of meaning and guidance through the ups and downs of an ordinary human life.

On the occasion of this second publication of the postscript, two retrospective observations come to mind—the first rather lengthy, the second quite brief.

I observe, first, an abrupt swerve in the postscript at the point where in its second-last paragraph I write:

Having thought for so long about the existential meaning of science in the stark and tragic terms of Russell, Camus, Monod, and Kolakowski, I confess that I experience a certain relief in thinking of play rather than explanation as quite plausibly the evolutionary taproot of religion.

The postscript then concludes with a move beyond play to a fragment of actual storytelling. This is the mini-fiction in which I imagine a boy (religion personified) saying to the boy Isaac Newton (science personified) on the beach where they have been playing together:

> "This has been fun, but it's getting dark, the tide is coming in, supper may be almost ready, and I'm going home. The ocean will still be there tomorrow. If you come along, I promise to tell you a story on the way."

Encroaching darkness, the incoming tide, hunger, and shelter are all existential concerns of the moment, collectively contrasted in this allegorical story-fragment with the ever-present ocean of ongoing possible investigation. But why, suddenly, this turn to play and then story?

Around the time when I delivered the final,

corrected draft of my general introduction to Julia Reidhead, then my editor at W. W. Norton and now president of the company, I had completed a lengthy review essay of the late Robert N. Bellah's *Religion in Human Evolution* (2011).[1] Toward the end of that immense and immensely impressive work, Bellah comes round to play as the aspect of the subject that, he confesses somewhat ruefully, he should have begun with. Play, by way of ritual, links even the most cerebral of theologies back to the earliest strata in human and prehuman behavior. So, thanks to Bellah, I had play as an archetypal human capacity on my mind as I completed my introduction. Yet what about story? What about the broader category of fiction, of which narrative fiction or story is, after all, only one variety? What about *that* form of playing around? Until this very last moment, I had somehow avoided the topic.

This surprises me in retrospect because fiction, and the suspension of disbelief that makes possible our imaginative participation in fiction, play so large a role in my 1995 book *God: A Biography* and its two sequels in a trilogy about God as a character in Jewish, Christian, and Muslim scripture. Earlier, even in this general introduction, I do say, if only in passing, "Religious truth can be conveyed as well through fiction as through history," but the general subject of fiction in religion and of fiction as, in itself, of potentially existential relevance seems in retrospect rather a glaring omission in my "unscholarly postscript," for—my own prior work quite aside—a major, if not *the* major, contemporary objection to religion is that it is founded on fiction and is therefore either simply false or suitable only for children.

But are not some fictions suitable and even indispensable for adults? Shortly after the decision was made to publish the general introduction to *The Norton Anthology of World Religions* as a separate short book, I read and was much engaged by Kwame Anthony Appiah's *As If: Idealization and Ideals* (2017). Appiah begins his brief but tightly argued book with a chapter entitled "Useful Untruths: Lessons from Hans Vaihinger." Vaihinger (1852–1933) was a German philosopher whose major work, first published in 1911, was translated into English in 1924 as *The Philosophy of "As If."* Appiah quotes approvingly an early, keynote sentence from this book: "It must be remembered that the object of the world of ideas as a whole is not the portrayal of reality—this would be an utterly impossible task—but rather to provide an *instrument for finding our way about more easily in the world.*"[2] Within the broad world of ideas, the object of religion, as distinct from either philosophy or science, would seem to be *par excellence* the provision of "an instrument for finding our way about more easily in the world." If "useful untruths" can have a place in philosophy and even in science, may they not also have a place in religion?

Vaihinger began, notably, in philosophical theology but moved on to the penetrating philosophical investigation of various other fields, including physics and economics. In all of them, he had grown keenly aware that myth or fiction was often undeniably functional. Appiah comments: "Vaihinger's suggestion that large areas of our thought are fictions amounts to this: Very often we can reasonably proceed as if what we know to be false is true *because it is useful for some purpose to do so.*"[3] There is nothing childish about doing this, nothing that must be outgrown as childhood passes.

In my postscript, I had imagined "human knowledge and ignorance as tracing a curve of asymptotic divergence, such that with every increase in knowledge, there occurs a greater increase in ignorance: the result is that our ignorance always exceeds our knowledge, and the gap between the two grows infinitely greater, not smaller, as infinite time passes." This was my private formulation of Vaihinger's assertion that "the portrayal of reality" is an "utterly impossible task," but my concern was exclusively with knowledge and ignorance rather than in any explicit way with fiction. Appiah is careful to note that Vaihinger does not wish to obliterate any and every distinction between reality and unreality or truth and falsehood, only to set aside or postpone the gargantuan task of a "full portrayal of reality" while applying what he called "fruitful errors" to the many smaller but urgent tasks at hand. His is an approach that I knew as instrumentalism in the philosophy of science. But Appiah, who does not use that term, finds much wider applicability for such "as if" thinking.

Where do we draw the line between belief and make-believe? When we honor the serious fictions of our greatest novelists, what is it that makes them serious? Why does the fact that they are fictitious not make them, by definition, unserious or suitable only for children? Does the difference not have something to do with their utility, to quote Vaihinger, as instruments "for finding our way about in the world"? But then why may some comparable utility not reside in the fictions carried forward by the world's religions? And how real is the prospect that any individual life or any collective human undertaking can succeed without employing one form of expeditious fiction or another?

An illustration here may be of some assistance. Consider the ringing words of Thomas Jefferson in the Declaration of Independence: "We hold these truths to be self-evident, that all men are created equal. . . ." Leave aside the biblical story implicit in the word "created" and attend only to the hallowed American belief in inherent human equality. Is it not empirically self-evident, against the Declaration of Independence, that all men are *not* born equal? Some are born rich, some poor; some into danger, others into safety; some are born beautiful and brilliant, others physically or mentally handicapped. What Jefferson proclaimed a self-evident truth is more accurately a self-evident fiction, one might only too reasonably object. But how different our American society would be if,

as in hereditary aristocracies, we honored the doctrine that inequality of birth rather than equality of dignity must shape society as its grounding
truth! Try proving the existence of human dignity. It's about as easy as proving the existence of
God. Yet the "useful fiction" of human equality, as
promulgated in the Declaration of Independence,
for all its unprovability, has been powerfully functional over time in making American society what
it is, and from that observation we may perhaps
infer that other fictions, including powerful religious fictions, can be comparably functional, even
when recognized as such, in shaping individual
and communal lives.

To pursue the analogy a little further, imagine three different stances or "faith postures"
toward Jefferson's belief in human equality. The
first posture would be that of the simple Jeffersonian believer. For him or her, no evidence need
be provided, for none is ever sought. The truth of
human equality is just taken for granted. The second stance would be that of the simple Jeffersonian
unbeliever. (Think, if you will, of Ayn Rand.) For
her or him, Jefferson's assertion of "self-evident"
equality is simply a rhetorical ploy to avoid fac-

ing the utter lack of empirical evidence for human equality, the abundance of empirical evidence for its opposite, and the practical conclusion that programs assuming or pursuing equality (and depriving the superior of what they deserve by nature) are sheer folly. The third stance would be that of the provisional believer. Without committing either to the final truth or the final falsehood of Jefferson's claim of inherent human equality, the provisional believer may proceed to the task of building and governing a society "as if" the claim were true, as if in some way all men (and all women) were indeed (created) equal.

Thus, in November 2018, Michael Bloomberg gave $1.8 billion to Johns Hopkins University to subsidize tuition at that university so that its admissions might thenceforth be "forever need-blind."[4] His Jeffersonian gift, as I choose to call it, is intended to mitigate the inequality among future students at Johns Hopkins that unequal wealth must otherwise inevitably create. Few can and fewer ever will do as much in dollar terms to support equality among Americans. Many indeed have used their wealth to foster inequality. Nonetheless other millions have employed and will continue to employ whatever means are at their disposal to bring American society into conformity with the truth of Jeffersonian faith—which may be a fiction—that "all men are created equal."

As it is for this secular American article of faith, so it may be as well for all forms of religious faith. Reserving judgment about ultimate truth or falsehood frees the provisional religious believer to proceed with a good will to religious practice, and just as practice is what has made the American republic what it is, so also practice is what has kept the religions as we know them surviving and often thriving despite much empirical evidence that their core contentions are fictitious. To claim this much is by no means to simply restate Pascal's famous wager, for success or failure in the task of "finding our way about more easily in the world" is one thing, reward or punishment in an afterlife quite another thing.

Where does this take us, or leave us? The thrust of Kwame Anthony Appiah's *As If* is that a wise, perhaps humbled admission of the place of fictions in a wide variety of legitimate or even indispensable human undertakings can bring us to a fuller, more self-conscious understanding of them and of ourselves as we are involved in them. Religion, though he notes the applicability of Vaihinger's thinking to it, is not one of the areas that Appiah explores. I am surprised in retrospect that I myself did not explore the place of fiction in the world's religions more than I did in my postscript. I should have done so not just for the reasons indicated above but also because the power of "as if" thinking so crucial to the functioning of fiction is cautionary as well as explanatory in the religious case. Any number of malignant prejudices may be accepted as provisionally true and then acted on in (as we revealingly put it) "good faith." Religion is the more powerful—and the study of religion the more relevant—because its operations can serve evil ends as readily as good.

But this brings me to my promised, brief second observation about that postscript. The point of the postscript was not to insinuate subjectively what I had announced earlier that we would not attempt objectively. The point, in other words, was not to slip in an entire philosophy of religion disguised as personal reminiscence. From anyone's interior dialogue about religion, however hasty or peremptory, an entire philosophy of religion can always be extrapolated, but such extrapolation was not the point in this instance. No, it was only to illustrate the place of the subjective in *every* engagement with religion.

In any case, I now have a minor confession to make about the shy religious story that I told in the prior edition. There, I mentioned that for some years I carried a skeptical quote from Bertrand Russell in my wallet—until my wallet was stolen. This was true, but in fact, I had carried two quotes in the lost wallet. The second, from a Japanese poet, did not make it into *The Norton Anthology of World Religions* because I thought at the time that I had lost it forever. I had forgotten the very name of the medieval Japanese master who wrote the words that had once so touched me. Later, after the anthology was in print, a kind American professor of Japanese and his intuitive Japanese wife patiently rediscovered the lost poem for me in a transliteration with a literal translation that I have adapted to be the epigraph to this book. Saigyō Hōshi says so much in his few words—so much both about agnosticism and skepticism and about the tears that follow when experience overflows all our capacities—that I can feel only embarrassment at my halting engagement with the same extremes. But such engagements are reasonable even when they must remain unfinished, and valuable, I must hope, even when they embarrass.

PREAMBLE:
ON STARTING FROM
WHERE WE ARE

The Western cast of mind, by any reckoning, has had a distorting effect in the practice as well as the study of religion as Western culture has become a world culture, and yet that very cast of mind has also had a liberating and fertilizing effect. A space has been created in which the religiously unknown and therefore incomparable has become known and comparable. Looking at the religions of others even from the outside but with a measure of openness, empathy, and good will can enable those of any religious tradition or none to see themselves from the outside as well, and that capacity is the very foundation of human sympathy and cultural wisdom. However clumsily attempted, the secular study of religion can open new worlds to the visitor's gaze.

In church one morning in the eighteenth century, the poet Robert Burns spotted a louse on a proper lady's bonnet and started thinking: If only she could see herself as he saw her! He went home and wrote his wonderfully earthy and witty "To a Louse, On Seeing One on a Lady's Bonnet, at Church 1786." The fun of the poem is that it is addressed to the louse in a mock "How dare you!" tone almost all the way to the end. At that point, however, it becomes suddenly reflective, even wistful, and Burns concludes, in his Scots English:

O wad some Pow'r the giftie gie us
To see oursels as ithers see us!
It wad frae monie a blunder free us,
    An' foolish notion:
What airs in dress an' gait wad lea'e us,
    An' ev'n Devotion!

Burns dreams, or half-prays, that some power would "the giftie gie us" (give us the gift) to see "oursels" (ourselves) as others see us—to see, as it were, the lice on our bonnets. Our fine and flouncing airs then "wad lea'e us" (would leave us). But it might not be simply vanity that would depart. The last words in the poem are "an' ev'n Devotion!" (and even devotion). Even our religious devotions might be affected if we could see ourselves at that moment just as others see us. So many of the cruelest mistakes in religion are made not out of malice but out of simple ignorance, blunders we would willingly avoid could we but see ourselves as others see us.

How religious do you have to be to undertake the study of religion? Is there a religious entrance requirement? I answer with another poem, this one by the contemporary American poet Todd Boss:

It Is Enough to Enter

the templar
halls of museums, for

example, or
the chambers of churches,

and admire
no more than the beauty

there, or
remember the graveness

of stone, or
whatever. You don't

have to do any
better. You don't have to

understand
the liturgy or know history

to feel holy
in a gallery or presbytery.

It is enough
To have come just so far.

You need not
be opened any more

Than does
A door, standing ajar.[5]

Strictly speaking, there is no entrance requirement for the study of religion; yet supposing that
you consider yourself essentially without religion,
you do have to "come just so far" toward linger-

ing with it. You have to be like "a door, standing ajar." You have to be as religious as that, but no more religious.

If it happens that you do recognize in yourself a connection or a loyalty to some one religious tradition, you need to be willing to look at parts of that tradition that you haven't thought about before or might even prefer not to think about. Looking at other traditions, you need to see the bonnet and not just the louse. Looking at your own, you need to see the louse as well the bonnet. You need to be as secular as that, but no more secular.

How religious is religious enough? How secular is secular enough? To quote an ancient Latin proverb, *Virtus stat in medio*: "Virtue stands in the middle." In that middling, muddling spirit, let us now begin.

CAN RELIGION BE DEFINED?

———

What is religion? The word exists in the English language, and people have some commonsense notion of what it refers to. Most understand it as one kind of human activity standing alongside other kinds, such as business, politics, warfare, art, law, sport, or science. Religion is available in a variety of forms, but what is it, really? What makes it itself?

Simple but searching questions like these may seem to be the starting point for the study of religion. Within the study of religion, they are more precisely the starting point for the *theory* of religion. And readers will not be surprised to learn that academic theoreticians of religion have not been content with the commonsense understanding of the subject.

The theoretical difficulties that attend any basic element of human thought or experience are undeniable. What is mathematics? What is art? What is law? What is music? Books have been written debating number theory, aesthetic theory, legal theory, and music theory. It should come as no surprise then that the theory of religion is no less actively debated than are those other theories. Some definitions of religion are so loose as to allow almost anything to qualify as a religion. Others are so strict as to exclude almost everything ordinarily taken to be a religion (prompting one recent contributor to the *Journal of the American Academy of Religion* to give his article the wry or rueful title "Religions: Are There Any?").[6]

The inconvenient truth is that no definition of religion now enjoys general acceptance. In *The Bonobo and the Atheist* (2013), the primatologist Frans de Waal writes:

> To delineate religion to everyone's satisfaction is hopeless. I was once part of a forum at the American Academy of Religion, when someone proposed we start off with a definition of religion. However much sense this made, the idea

was promptly shot down by another participant, who reminded everyone that last time they tried to define religion half the audience had angrily stomped out of the room. And this in an academy named after the topic![7]

A survey of competing theories, if we were to attempt one here, could quickly jump to twenty-three entries if we simply combined the contents of two recent American handbooks—the eight in Daniel L. Pals's *Eight Theories of Religion* (2006) and the fifteen in Michael Stausberg's *Contemporary Theories of Religion: A Critical Companion* (2009).[8]

Though no one writing on religion can entirely escape theoretical commitments, *The Norton Anthology of World Religions* is foremost an anthology of primary texts. By the term *primary* its editors understand texts produced by the practitioners of each of the anthologized religions for their fellow practitioners. Such an anthology does not collect theories of religion, for the simple reason that such theories are secondary texts. They belong not to the creation and practice of religion but, retrospectively, to its study and analysis. Accordingly, they have rarely been of much interest to religious practitioners themselves.

Religious practitioners are far from unique in this regard. "Philosophy of science is about as useful to scientists as ornithology is to birds," Richard Feynman (1918–1988), a Caltech physicist, famously quipped.[9] The philosophy (or theory) of religion is of as little use to, say, the Buddhist as philosophy of science is to the scientist. Just as the scientist is interested in her experiment rather than in the philosophy of science and the painter in his painting rather than in the philosophy of art, so the Buddhist is interested in the Buddha rather than in the philosophy of religion. The term *religion* itself, as an academic term comprising—as indeed it does in this work—many different religious traditions, may not be of much practical utility to the practitioner of any one of the traditions.

And yet scholarship at its most empirical cannot escape theory, because, to quote a dictum from the philosophy of science, all data are theory-laden. A theory of some sort will be found operative even when no explicit theoretical commitment has been made.

If, then, some tacit theory or theories of religion must necessarily have informed the choices made by the associate editors of *The Norton Anthology of*

World Religions, given the general editor's decision to impose no single theory, did any silent theoretical convergence occur? Once the results were in and the editors' choices had actually been made, did they reflect a working answer to the question "What is religion?"

As general editor, I believe that they did and do, though it would take some rather elaborate spelling out to explain just *how* they do. Something more modest but more readily discernible must suffice here—namely, the claim that the choices made by the respective associate editors reflect a common method or, more modestly still, a common approach to the task of presenting a major religious literature with some coherence. In brief, the six associate editors have approached the six religions whose texts they anthologize as six kinds of practice rather than as six kinds of belief. In common usage, religious and unreligious people are divided into "believers" and "unbelievers." The editors have departed from this common usage, proceeding instead on the silent and admittedly modest premise that religion is as religion *does*. Even when speaking of belief, as they do only occasionally, they generally treat it as embedded in practice and inseparable from practice. Monotheism in the abstract is a belief. "Hear, O Israel, the Lord is our God, the Lord alone" as sung by a cantor in a synagogue is a practice.

When religion is approached as practice, what follows? Clearly, Daoist practice, Muslim practice, Christian practice, and so on are not identical, but the substantial differences *within* each of them can loom as large as the differences from one to another among them. *The goal of* The Norton Anthology of World Religions *is to present through texts how this variety has developed and how the past continues to shape the present.* Thus, the body of material put on exhibit in the anthology serves less to answer the question "What is religion?" in any theoretically elaborate or definitive way than to question the answers others have given to that question—answers such as those offered by, for example, the twenty-three theories alluded to above. Whatever fascinating questions a given theory of religion may have posed and answered to its own satisfaction, it must also, we submit, be able to account for the complexity of the data that these primary texts exhibit. In the meantime, the working focus is squarely on practice.

To illustrate, here is part of the answer that Wendy Doniger, the anthology's Hinduism editor, gives to the question "What is Hinduism?":

Some scholars have tried to identify a cluster of beliefs and practices that are important but not essential to Hinduism; not every Hindu will believe in all the ideas or follow all the practices, but each Hindu will adhere to some combination of them, as a non-Hindu would not. Scholars differ as to the number and nature of the elements of this cluster, but they should combine aspects of both the literary tradition and popular Hinduism: belief in the ancient sacred texts called the Vedas (which excludes Buddhism and Jainism); *karma* (the doctrine of actions that determine one's reincarnation, which does not exclude Buddhism and Jainism); *dharma* (Hindu religion, law, and justice, different from Buddhist *dhamma*); a cosmology centered around Mount Meru; devotion (*bhakti*) to one or more members of an extensive pantheon; the ritual offering (*puja*) of fruit and flowers to a deity; sacrificial offerings of butter into a fire; vegetarianism as an ideal, if not necessarily a practice; nonviolence and blood sacrifice (which

may or may not be mutually exclusive); pilgrimage; offerings to snakes; worship of local gods and
goddesses; worship at shrines of Muslim saints;
and so forth. This polythetic approach could be
represented by a Venn diagram, a chart made
of intersecting circles. It might be grouped into
sectors of different colors, one for beliefs or practices that some Hindus shared with Buddhists and
Jains, another largely confined to Hindu texts in
Sanskrit (the ancient literary language of India), a
third more characteristic of popular worship and
practice, and so forth. But since there is no single
central quality that all Hindus must have, the
emptiness in the center suggests that the figure in
the center might better be named a Zen diagram,
a Venn diagram that has no central ring.[10]

Venn diagrams are named after John Venn
(1834–1923), the British logician and mathematician
who used diagrams of intersecting circles to illustrate set theory. In Doniger's discussion, the set in
question is a mingled set of Hindu religious practices and beliefs, a kind of repertory from which
different Hindus and different groups of Hindus
will be found to choose different subsets. Some of

these practices are simple enough to be within the reach of the illiterate. Others have challenged the minds of philosophers for centuries. As for that one practice or belief that might truly *define* Hinduism, the way a backbone defines a vertebrate, Doniger speaks for many in her field when she declines to single out any one such belief or practice. The central spot in her imaginary diagram that would be occupied by that "essence of Hinduism" is an empty space. And since emptiness is a category famous in Zen Buddhism, Doniger playfully calls her imaginary Venn diagram of Hinduism a Zen diagram.

Doniger's list is long, but its length is material to the point she makes, for she characterizes her working definition of Hinduism as *polythetic*, using a word that is to be heard in contrast with *monothetic*. A monothetic approach to Hinduism would insist on doing just what Doniger declines to do. It would define an "essence of Hinduism," place it in the central space that she deliberately leaves empty, and build out from there. As she notes, many Hinduism scholars now prefer a polythetic approach like hers. They are prepared to recognize many Hinduisms, many group or individual *syntheses* confected from polythetically available beliefs and practices, while retaining the collective term *Hinduism* simply for its academic convenience. Many other -*ism*s and equivalent terms do turn up within what we now call Hinduism studies—arcane terms such as *Brahmanism*, *Vaishnavism*, *Advaita*, and so forth. But if the word *Hinduism* were retired, then some other term would be needed to refer to the ways in which all these -*ism*s overlap. There is a whiff of essentialism about every common noun in the language, but, alas, we cannot retire language itself.

Every major religion has contained multiple versions of itself both over time and at any given time, and the anthology does not attempt to drive past the multiplicity to the singular essence of the thing. Practitioners, of course, have not always been so neutral. Many have been or still are prepared to deny the legitimacy of others as Hindu, Muslim, Christian, and so on. But over time, those denials themselves simply become a part of the broader story.

Just as there is no Hinduism as such but only a polythetic array of practices that may be differently combined, so there may be no religion as such but only a far greater array of practices that, again, may be differently combined, not just within recognized religious traditions but across them. Thus, Doniger lists "worship at shrines of Muslim saints" as a practice that "some Hindus" engage in without ceasing to be Hindus. Syncretism, the introduction of a feature from one religion into the life of another, is in itself an argument that the borrower and the lender are, or can be, related even when they are not, and never will be, identical. Multiple religious belonging—double or triple affiliation—sometimes takes syncretism a step further. And while borrowings across major borders are an additive process, adjustments within borders can often be a subtractive process, as seen in many statements that take the form "I am a Buddhist, but . . . ," "I am a Catholic, but . . . ," "I am a Muslim, but . . . ," and so forth. In such statements, the speaker takes the broad term as a starting point and then qualifies it until it fits properly.

Yet I do not claim anything more than practical utility for this default approach to the subject. Just as Doniger declines to define the essence of Hinduism en route to a richly furnished introduction to Hindu literature, so a good many scholars of religion decline to define the essence of religion itself but do not find themselves inhibited by that abstention from saying a great deal of interest about one religious tradition or another. Rather than monothetically name at the outset the one feature that establishes the category *religion* before discussing the particular religion that interests them, they make the usually silent assumption that the full range of beliefs and practices that have been conventionally thought of as religious is vast and that each religion must be allowed to do as it does, assembling its subsets from the never-to-be-fully-enumerated full roster of world religious practices. Having made that assumption, the scholars take a deep breath and go on to talk about what they want to talk about.

The respective Venn diagrams of each tradition, in this definition-by-abstention, overlap to varying degrees with the Venn diagrams of the others. How much coherence is there in any one diagram, and how much in the ensemble? Can they be comprehended as a coherent system? Twenty-first-century religion scholars are prepared to acknowledge coherence when they find it but determined never to impose it. They are aware that the entries made under the heading *religion* may not all be versions of just the same thing, but they are equally aware that the overlaps, the innumerable ad hoc points of contact, are also there and also real—and so they find the continued use of the collective term *religion* justified for the enriching and enlightening comparisons that it facilitates. All knowledge begins with comparison.

In telling the life stories of six major, living, international religions through their respective primary texts, the editors of *The Norton Anthology of World Religions* neither suppress variability over time in service to any supposedly timeless essence of the thing nor, even when using the word *classical*, dignify any one age as truly golden. Each of the stories ends with modernity, but modernity in each case is neither the climax nor the denouement of the story. It is not the last chapter, only the latest.

HOW CHRISTIAN
EUROPE LEARNED TO
COMPARE RELIGIONS

M ost people, we said earlier, understand religion as "one kind of human activity standing alongside other kinds, such as business, politics,
warfare, art, law, sport, or science." Another way to
say this is that they understand religion to be one
domain among many, each separate from the others.
Wendy Doniger's definition of Hinduism is broadly
compatible with this popular understanding. So is a
widely influential definition of religion formulated
by the anthropologist Clifford Geertz (1926–2006).

In "Religion as a Cultural System," first published in 1966, Geertz defined religion as

> *(1) a system of symbols which acts to (2) establish
> powerful, pervasive, and long-lasting moods and*

motivations in men by (3) formulating conceptions
of a general order of existence and (4) clothing these
conceptions with such an aura of factuality that (5)
the moods and motivations seem uniquely realistic.[11]

Geertz does not claim that all cultures are equally
religious. In fact, toward the end of his essay he
observes that "the degree of religious articulate-
ness is not a constant even as between societies
of similar complexity."[12] However, he does tacitly
assume that religion is if not universal then at least
extremely widespread and that it is a domain separate from others, such as—to name two that he
explores—science and ideology.[13]

But just how widespread is religion, and is it
truly a domain separable from the rest of culture?
Can religion really be distinguished from ideology? In Geertz's terms, wouldn't Marxism qualify
as a religion? In recent decades, some have argued
that even a thoroughly secular anthropologist like
Geertz, in whose definition of religion neither God
nor Christ is mentioned, can be seen as carrying
forward an ideological understanding of religion
that originated in the Christian West and has lived
on in Western academic life as a set of inadequately

examined assumptions. That religion is a domain separate from either ethnicity or culture is one of two key, historically Christian assumptions. That religion is a universal phenomenon—in some form, a part of every human society and even every human mind—is the other key assumption.

Perhaps the most widely cited historical critique of these assumptions is Tomoko Masuzawa's revealing *The Invention of World Religions, Or, How European Universalism Was Preserved in the Language of Pluralism* (2005). Masuzawa's book is not about the invention of the world's religions themselves but about the invention of *world religions* as a phrase used in the West to talk about them, postulating their parallel existence as separable and separate realities, available as an indefinitely expandable group for academic discussion.[14]

When and how, she asks, did this omnibus-phrase *world religions* come into the general usage that it now enjoys? She concludes her influential investigation with the candid confession that the invention and, especially, the very widespread adoption of the phrase remain something of a puzzle—but her analysis traces the usage back only to the nineteenth century. Our claim below is that though the phrase *world religions* may be recent, its roots run much deeper than the nineteenth century, as deep in fact as early Christianity's peculiar and unprecedented self-definition.

To say this is not to undercut the strength of the criticism. Christian explorers, traders, missionaries, and colonists encountering non-Western societies, especially after the discovery of the Americas and the colonial expansion of the West into Asia, have often isolated and labeled as "religions" behaviors that they took to be the local equivalents of what they knew in the West as Christianity. This process of isolating and labeling was a mistake when and if the societies themselves did not understand the behaviors in question as constituting either a separate domain or merely one instance of a more general phenomenon called religion. Moreover, when those purporting to understand non-Western societies in these historically Christian terms were invaders and imperialists, a perhaps unavoidable theoretical mistake could have grievous practical consequences. And when, in turn, ostensibly neutral, secular theories of religion—not imposed by conquerors or missionaries but merely proffered by Western academics—are alleged to make the same historically Christian assumptions, the entire project of comparative religious study may be challenged as Christian imperialism.

Because the viability and indeed the enormous value of such study were premises of *The Norton Anthology of World Religions,* the imperialism challenge called for a significant response, one that necessarily included substantial attention to just how Christianity had influenced the study of what the West has defined as world religions. The intention in what follows, however, is by no means to make a case for Christianity as inherently central or supreme among the world's religions. We intend rather, and only, to trace how, in point of fact, Christianity began as central to the Western *study* of religions and then, by degrees, yielded its position as more polycentric forms of study emerged.

Let us begin by stipulating that Christians did indeed acquire very early and thereafter never entirely lost the habit of thinking of their religion as a separate domain. Once this is conceded, it should come as no great surprise that as a corollary of this habit, they should have adopted early and never entirely lost the habit of thinking of other religions, rightly or wrongly, as similarly separate domains. This would be simply one more instance of the human habit of beginning with the known and with the self and working outward to the unknown and to the others.

But we must stipulate further that Christians made a second assumption—namely, that theirs should become humankind's first-ever programmatically "world" religion. The idea of universally valid religious truth was not new in itself. Ancient Israel had long since been told that its vocation was to be the light of the world. In the book of Isaiah, God says to his people through the prophet (49:6):

> It is too light a thing that you should be my servant to raise up the tribes of Jacob and to restore the preserved of Israel; I will give you as a light to the nations, that my salvation may reach to the end of the earth.[15]

In the Gospel of Matthew, Jesus turns this latent potential into a radically intrusive program for action. His final words to his apostles are

> Go therefore, and make disciplines of *all nations*, baptizing them in the name of the Father and of

the Son and of the Holy Spirit, teaching them
to observe all that I have commanded you; and,
lo, I am with you always, even to the close of
the age. (Matthew 28:19–20; emphasis added.)

How ever did this instruction, as the first Christians put it into practice, lead to the secular study
of "world religions" as we know it today?

The Social Oddity of
the Early Church

In the earliest centuries of its long history, the
Christian church defined its belief as different from
the official polytheism of the Roman Empire, on
the one hand, and from the monotheism of Rabbinic Judaism, on the other, inasmuch as the
rabbinic Jews did not recognize Jesus as God incarnate. But if the church was thus, to borrow a con-
venient phrase from contemporary American life,
a faith-based organization, it was not just a school
of thought: it was also an *organization*. As faith-
based, it undeniably placed unique and unprecedented stress on belief (and indeed set the pattern
by which today all those religiously active in any

way are routinely called *believers*, even when not all regard belief as central to their practice). Yet as an organization, the church depended not just on a distinct set of beliefs but also on a social identity separate, on the one hand, from that of the Roman Empire (or any other empire) and equally separate, on the other, from that of the Jewish nation (or any other nation). As a faith-based, voluntary, non-profit, multiethnic nongovernmental organization, the Christian church was a social novelty: nothing quite like it had ever been seen before. And as Christians, growing steadily in number, projected their novel collective self-understanding upon Roman and Jewish social reality alike, the effect was profoundly disruptive. Though many others would follow, these were the first two instances of Christian projection, and an analysis of how they worked is especially instructive.

By encouraging Roman polytheists to *convert* to Christianity while maintaining that they did not thereby cease to be Romans, the Christians implicitly asserted convertibility itself. The term *religion* did not exist then in Greek, Latin, or Aramaic as a fully developed universal category containing both Roman polytheism and Christianity, but in the very action of conversion the future category was already implicit. By seeking to convert Roman polytheists to Christianity, the early Christians implied that Roman religiosity was a domain both separate from the rest of Roman life and replaceable. You could leave your Roman religiosity behind, as the very act of conversion demonstrated, while bringing the rest of your Roman identity with you.

In the first century, conversion thus defined was an unprecedented and socially disruptive novelty. Until the destabilizing intrusion of Christianity, respect for the Roman gods had always been inseparable from simply being Roman: religious identity and civic identity had always constituted an unbroken whole. Christianity encouraged Romans to split that single identity into a double identity: religion, on the one hand; culture and ethnicity, on the other. In this sequestration of the religiously meaningful from the religiously neutral or meaningless were born, on the one hand, religion as Western modernity has come to understand it— religion as involving some semblance of faith and some form of collective identity separable from ethnicity or culture—and, on the other hand, the very possibility of secular culture.

In by far the most important instance of this division of social identity, the original Christian Jews, having adopted a minority understanding of Jewish tradition, denied that they were any less Jewish for that reason. First-century Jewry would not have disagreed had the matter stopped there, for there were many peacefully coexisting Jewish views about Jewish belief and practice. As no more than the latest variation on the old themes, the Christian Jews would not have created anything structurally new. But they did create something new by taking the further step of bringing themselves, with their recognizably Jewish religious views (views indeed unrecognizable as anything except Jewish), into an unprecedented social relationship with non-Jews—namely, into the newborn Christian church. By linking themselves to non-Jews in this way without renouncing their Jewish identity, the Christian Jews—enjoying particular success in the Roman Diaspora—demonstrated that as they conceived their own Jewish religiosity to be distinguishable from their Jewish culture and ethnicity, so they conceived the same two components of identity to be likewise distinguishable for all other Jews.

Rabbinic Judaism, dominant in Palestine and the Mesopotamian Diaspora, would eventually repudiate this Christian projection and reassert that Jewish religiosity and Jewish ethnicity are one and indistinguishable. In the rabbinic view that became and has remained dominant in world Judaism, there are no "Judaists," only Jews. But this reassertion did not happen overnight: it took generations, even centuries. Neither the Romans nor the Jews nor the Christians themselves immediately understood the full novelty of what was coming into existence.

Through most of world history, in most parts of the world, what we are accustomed to call religion, ethnicity, and culture have been inextricable parts of a single whole. How did Christianity begin to become an exception to this general rule? On the one hand, it appropriated a set of Jewish religious ideas—including monotheism, revelation, covenant, scripture, sin, repentance, forgiveness, salvation, prophecy, messianism, and apocalypticism—without adopting the rest of the Jewish way of life. On the other hand, it universalized these Jewish religious ideas, creating a new social entity, the church, through which non-Jews could be initiated into an enlarged version of the ancestral Jewish covenant with God. The Jews had believed for centuries God's declaration, "I am the LORD your God, who have separated you from the peoples" (Leviticus 20:24) and "you are a people holy to the LORD your God" (Deuteronomy 7:6). In effect, the Christian Jews split the idea of covenanted separateness and holiness from what consequently became the relatively secularized idea of nationality. The Jews were still a people, they maintained, but God had now revised and universalized the terms of his covenant. In the words of Jesus' apostle Peter, "Truly I perceive that God shows no partiality, but in every nation any one who fears him and does what is right is acceptable to him" (Acts 10:34–35).

The original Greek word for church, *ekklēsia*, suggests a collective understanding of church members as "called out" from other kinds of religious, ethnic, or political membership into this new—and now, in principle, universal—"people set apart as holy." The *ekklēsia* offered its members a sense of sacred peoplehood, but it tellingly lacked much else that ordinarily maintains a national identity. It had no ancestral land, no capital city, no language of its own, no literature at the start other than what it had inherited from the Jews, no distinct cuisine, no standard dress, and no political or governmental support beyond the organizational management of the church itself. Moreover, this ethnically mixed group was atheist in its attitude toward all gods except the God of Israel as they had come to understand him—God as incarnate in Jesus the Messiah. Within the political culture of the Roman Empire, this rejection of the empire's gods was a seditious and rebellious rejection of Roman sovereignty itself. When, unsurprisingly, the empire recognized it as such and began intermittently to persecute the church, the Christian sense of separateness only grew.

In this form, and despite intermittent persecution, the church grew quietly but steadily for more than three centuries. At that point, with perhaps a fifth of the population of the Roman Empire enrolled in separate local Christian churches under relatively autonomous elected supervisors (bishops), the emperor Constantine (r. 312–37) first legalized Christianity and then stabilized its doctrine by requiring the Christian bishops—ordered to convene for the first time as a council at Nicaea, near his eventual capital city of Constantinople—to define it. In 381, the emperor Theodosius (r. 379–95) made this newly defined Christianity the official religion of the Roman Empire, and the new religion—no longer persecuted but now operating under a large measure of imperial control—began a fateful reversal of course. It began to fuse with the political governance and the Hellenistic culture of imperial Rome, compromising the character of the *ekklēsia* as a domain separate from nationality or culture. In a word, it began to normalize.

The establishment of Christianity as the state religion of the Roman Empire ushered in a period of rapid growth, pushed by the government, within the borders of the empire. Beyond them, however, most notably in the Persian Empire just to the east, its new status had the opposite effect. Once relatively unhindered as a social movement taken to be as compatible with Persian rule as with Roman, Christianity now became suspect as the official religion of the enemy.

Meanwhile, in Rome itself—the "First Rome," as historically prior to the Eastern Empire's capital, Constantinople—and in the western European territories that it administered, a partial but significant return to the original, culturally abnormal separation of domains occurred just a century later. In 476, Odoacer, king of an invading Germanic tribe, deposed the last Roman emperor, Romulus Augustulus, without effectively assuming authority over the Christian church. Instead, the power of the bishop of Rome—the highest surviving official of the old imperial order—over the church in western Europe began to grow, while the power of kings and feudal lords over all that was not the church steadily grew as well. The nominally unified imperial authority over the empire and its established religion thus split apart. To be sure, for centuries the pope claimed the authority to anoint kings to their royal offices, and at certain moments this was a claim that could be sustained. But gradually, a sense that civilian and religious authority were different and separate began to set in. At the same time, the identity of the church as, once again, detached or disembedded from the state and from culture alike—the church as a potentially universal separate domain, a holy world unto itself—began to consolidate.

The Four-Cornered Medieval
Map of Religion

Wealth, power, and population in the world west of India were concentrated during the sixth century in the Persian Empire and in the Eastern Roman or Byzantine Empire. Western Europe during the same century—all that had once been the Western Roman Empire—was far poorer, weaker, more sparsely populated, and culturally more isolated than the empires to its east. Then, during the seventh and eighth centuries, a third major power arose. Arabia had long provided mercenary soldiers to both of the then-dominant empires; but religiously inspired by the Islam newly preached by Muhammad (ca. 570–632) and militarily unified under his successors, it became a major world power in its own right with stunning speed. Arab armies conquered the entirety of the Persian Empire within a generation. Within a century, they had taken from the Eastern Roman Empire its Middle Eastern and North African possessions (half of its total territory) as well as the major Mediterranean islands. From what had been the Western Roman Empire, they had subtracted three-quarters of Spain and penetrated deep into France until driven back across the Pyrenees by the unprecedented European alliance that defeated them in the 732 Battle of Poitiers.

The political map of the world had been redrawn from India to the Atlantic, but what of the religious map? How did western European Christians now understand themselves among the religions of the world? The symbolic birth date of Europe as Christendom has long been taken to be Christmas Day of the year 800. On that date, Pope Leo III crowned Charles the Great, better known as Charlemagne—the grandson of Charles Martel, who had unified the European forces at Poitiers— as the first "Holy Roman Emperor." The Muslim invasion from distant Arabia had shocked an isolated and fragmented region into an early assertion of common religious and geographical identity. As a result, there was a readiness to give political expression to a dawning collective self-understanding. The lost Western Roman Empire was by no means reconstituted: Charlemagne was an emperor without much of an empire, his coronation expressing a vision more than a reality. But the vision itself mattered decisively in another way, for what came into existence at about this time was an understood quadripartite map of the world of religion that would remain standard in Europe for centuries.

There was, first and foremost for Christians, Christianity itself: the Christian church understood to be the same single, separate domain wherever it was found, with the same distinct relationship to national and cultural identity. To the extent that it rested on common faith, the church could be divided by heresy; but even heretical Christians, of whom there would be fewer in the early ninth century than there had been in earlier Christian centuries, were still understood to be Christians. They were practicing the right religion in a wrong way, but they were not practicing another religion altogether.

There was, second, Judaism: the Jews of Europe, a population living among Christians, disparaged but well known, whose relationship to Christianity was well remembered and whose religious authenticity rested on a recognized if more or less resented prior relationship with the same God that the Christians worshipped. Christian understanding of Jewish religious life as the Jews actually lived it was slender, and Christian knowledge of the vast rabbinic literature that had come into existence between the second and the ninth century, much of it in far-off Mesopotamia, was virtually nonexistent. Knowledge of Greek had been lost in Latin Europe, and knowledge of the Hebrew and Aramaic that the Jews of Europe had managed to preserve (despite recurrent persecution) was confined to them alone. Yet, this ignorance notwithstanding, Christian Europe was well aware that the Jews practiced a religion different from their own. And the implicit Christian understanding of religion as a separate domain of potentially universal extent was reinforced by the fact that from the outside, Jewish religious practice appeared to be at least as deeply divorced from national and cultural practices as was Christian religious practice: the Jews, who had lost their land and were dispersed around the world, lived in Europe much as Europe's Christians lived.

The third corner of Europe's four-cornered understanding of world religion was Islam, though the terms *Islam* and *Muslim* would not come into European usage until centuries later. Even the term *Arab* was not standard. The multinational religious commonwealth that we now call world Islam has been traditionally referred to by the Muslims themselves with the Arabic expression *dar al-islam*, the "House of Islam" or the "House of Submission" (because *islam* means "submission"— that is, submission to God). Whether it was *Saracen*, *Moor*, *Turk*, or *Arab*, the ethnic terms used by Christians to refer to the Muslims who faced them in the south and the east depended on time and place. Christendom as the Holy Roman Empire had become a domain geographically separate from the House of Islam. Similarly, Christianity as distinct from Christendom was evidently a domain of belief and practice distinguishable from Islam. But among Christians, the further inference was that as Christian identity was separate from Bavarian or Florentine identity, so Muslim identity must be separate from Arab or Turkish identity. To some extent, this was a false inference, for obligatory Arabic in the Qur'an and obligatory pilgrimage to Mecca did much to preserve the originally Arab identity of Islam. Yet the tricontinental distribution and ethnic variability of the House of Islam fostered among Europeans an understanding of Islam as, like Christianity, a potentially universal religion separable from the ethnicity of any one of its component parts.

As Christian anxiety mounted that the year 1000 might mark the end of the world (an outcome that some Christians saw predicted in the New Testament book of Revelation), Muhammad came to be seen by some as the Antichrist, a destructive figure whose appearance during the last apocalyptic period before the end had been foretold (again in the book of Revelation). Yet gradually, albeit as "Mohammedanism," Islam came to be differentiated from Christianity in theological rather than in such floridly mythological terms. The Qur'an was translated into Latin in 1142. The High Middle Ages began to witness various forms of religious and cultural encounter—some as an unintended consequence of the Crusades; others through the influence of large Christian minorities living under Muslim rule and, over time, substantial Muslim minorities living under Christian rule, notably in Spain and Sicily. Finally, there was the mediating influence of a cross-culturally significant Jewish population residing on either side of the Muslim–Christian border and communicating across it. One result of these minglings was a gradually growing overlap in the techniques in use in all three communities for the exegesis of the sacred scriptures that for each mattered so much.

As Muslim monotheism came gradually into clearer focus, medieval Christianity came to recognize Muslims as worshippers of the same God that Jews and Christians worshipped. Meanwhile, Islam was, like Christianity, a religion that actively sought converts who were then made part of a separate quasi-national, quasi-familial, yet potentially universal social entity. The genesis of the Western understanding of religion as such—religion as a separate but expandable social category—was thus significantly advanced by Christianity's encounter with another social entity so like itself in its universalism and its relative independence from ethnic or cultural identity.

The fourth corner of the world religion square was occupied by a ghost—namely, the memory of long-dead Greco-Roman polytheism. Christianity was born among the urban Jews of the Roman Empire and spread gradually into the countryside. Even in largely rural Europe, monasteries functioned as surrogate cities and Christianity spread outward from these centers of structure and literacy. *Pagus* is the Latin word for "countryside," and in the countryside the old polytheisms lingered long after they had died out in the cities. Thus, a rural polytheist was a *paganus*, and *paganismus* (paganism) became synonymous with polytheism. In England, pre-Christian polytheism lingered in the inhospitable heath, and so *heathenism* became an English synonym for *paganism*. Though polytheism is not necessarily idolatrous (one may believe in many gods without making a single idol), polytheistic belief and idolatrous practice were generally conflated. More important for the centuries that lay ahead, the increasingly jumbled memory of what Greco-Roman polytheism—remembered as "paganism"—had been in the Christian past was projected upon the enormous and almost entirely unknown world beyond the realms occupied by Christians, Muslims, and Jews.

The quadripartite typology just sketched was only one long-lived stage in the development of the comparative study of religion in Christian Europe. We may pause to note, however, that as of the year 800 Judaism and Islam were operating under similar typologies. The Qur'an, definitive for all Islamic thought, takes frequent and explicit note of Judaism and Christianity, while the place occupied by the memory of Greco-Roman polytheism in Christianity is occupied in the Qur'an by the memory of polytheism as it existed in Arabia at the time when Muhammad began to receive his revelations. World Jewry, as a minority maintaining its identity and its religious practice in both Christendom and the House of Islam, had a richer experience of both Christians and Muslims than either of those two had of the other. Yet what functioned for Jews in the way that the memory of Greco-Roman polytheism functioned for Christians and the memory of Arabian polytheism functioned for Muslims was the memory of ancient Canaanite, Philistine, and Babylonian polytheism as recorded in the Bible and used thereafter as a template for understanding all those who were the enemies of God and the persecutors of his Chosen People.

Now, the comparison of two religions on terms set by one of them is like the similarly biased comparison of two nationalities: the outcome is a predictable victory for the side conducting the comparison. In fact, when religion and ethnicity are fused, religious comparison is commonly stated in ethnic terms rather than in what we would consider religious terms. Thus, in the Hebrew Bible, apostasy from the religion of Israel is called "*foreign worship*" (*'avodah zarah*) rather than simply false worship, though falsehood or worse is unmistakably implied. To the extent that ethnicity is taken to be a matter of brute fact, and therefore beyond negotiation, religion bound to ethnicity has seemed a nonnegotiable matter of fact as well.

In this regard, however, the condition of medieval Christian Europe was interestingly unstable. Demographically, the two largest religious realities it knew—Islam and Christianity itself—were consciously and ideologically multinational in character, and both actively sought converts from all nations. Judaism was not evangelistic in this way, but world Jewry was uniquely the world's first global nation: the bulk of its population was distributed internationally in such a way that Jews were accustomed in every place to distinguish their ethnicity from the ethnicity of the locale and their religion from its religion. Christian prejudice often prevented Jewish acculturation (not to suppose that Jews always wished to acculturate), but it did not always do so. And so during extended periods of Christian toleration, even the generally firm Jewish sense that religion, ethnicity, and culture were a seamless whole may have become more difficult to sustain. This three-sided—Christian, Muslim, and Jewish—embrace of the notion that religion was a separate domain set the stage in Europe for the comparison of the three on terms derived from a neutral fourth entity that was not to be equated with any one of them.

This fourth entity was Aristotelian philosophy as recovered in Europe during the eleventh and twelfth centuries. Of course, the philosophical discussions that began to be published—such as Abelard's mid-twelfth-century *Dialogue among a Philosopher, a Jew, and a Christian*, in which the philosopher of the title often appears to be a Muslim—always ended in victory for the imagined Christian. Yet Abelard (1079–1142) was eventually condemned by the church because his dialogue clearly recognized reason, mediated by philosophy, as independent of the religions being discussed and as capable of rendering judgments upon them all. Philosophy as that fourth, neutral party would be joined over time by psychology, sociology, anthropology, economics, evolutionary biology, cognitive science, and other analytical tools. But these enlargements lay centuries in the future. As the

Middle Ages were succeeded by the Renaissance,
philosophy had made a crucial start toward making
neutral comparisons, even though Europe's quadripartite map of the world's religions was still quite
firmly in place, with most comparisons still done
on entirely Christian and theological terms.

The Renaissance Rehearsal of Comparative Religion

The Italian Renaissance—beginning in the four-
teenth century and flourishing in the fifteenth
and sixteenth—is commonly taken to be more
important as a movement in art and literature than
in philosophy or religion. To be sure, it did not
attempt a transformation of European Christianity
comparable to that of the Protestant Reformation
of the sixteenth century. But the kind of religious
comparison that began in the early eighteenth
century, in the aftermath of Europe's devastating
seventeenth-century Protestant–Catholic Wars of
Religion, was foreshadowed during the Renaissance by the revival of classical Greek and Latin and
by the recovery of masterpieces of world literature
written in those languages.

First of all, perfected knowledge of Latin and the recovered knowledge of Greek enabled Italian scholars to publish critical editions of the texts of classical antiquity as well as philologically grounded historical criticism of such later Latin texts as the Donation of Constantine, exposed as a papal forgery by the Italian humanist Lorenzo Valla (1407–1457). It was in Renaissance Italy, too, that Christian Europe first recovered knowledge of biblical Hebrew. The earliest chair of Hebrew was established late in the fifteenth century at the University of Bologna. Despite repeated persecutions, ghettoizations, and expulsions, the Jewish population of Italy grew substantially during the Renaissance, enthusiastically embracing the then-new technology of printing with movable type. The first complete publication of the Hebrew Bible in the original, with Jewish commentaries, appeared in Venice in 1517 and proved highly instructive to Christian Europe; by the end of the following century, Italian scholars were even starting to read both the post-biblical rabbinic literature and the Kabbalah, writings in a later extra-rabbinic Jewish mystical tradition that fascinated some of them. Little by little, Christian Europe was beginning to learn from Europe's Jews.

As the Renaissance began to introduce Christian Europe by slow degrees to the critical examination of ancient texts as well as to the inner religious life of Judaism, it accomplished something similar in a more roundabout way for the lost religions of Greece and Rome. The humanists of the Renaissance did not believe in the gods and goddesses of Olympus as they believed in God the Almighty Father of Christianity, but even as they read the classical literature only as literature, they nonetheless were taken deep inside the creedal, ritual, imaginative, and literary life of another religion—namely, the lost Greco-Roman polytheism. During the Italian Renaissance, the term *humanist* (Italian *umanista*), we should recall, was not used polemically, as if in some sort of pointed contrast to *theist*. Rather, it was a declaration of allegiance to the humanizing, civilizing power of art and imaginative literature. Renaissance humanism's imaginative engagement with the religions of classical Greece and Rome thus constituted an unplanned rehearsal for the real-world, real-time imaginative engagements with non-Christian religions and cultures that lay immediately and explosively ahead for Europe. When the Spanish *conquistadores* encountered the living polytheism of Aztec Mexico, their first interpretive instinct was to translate the gods of Tenochtitlán into their nearest Greek and Roman equivalents. This was an intellectually clumsy move, to be sure, but less clumsy than interpreting them exclusively in monotheist Christian terms would have been. Moreover, because neither classical paganism nor Aztec polytheism was taken to be true, the two could be compared objectively or, if you will, humanistically—and from that early and fumbling act of comparison many others would follow.

In the study of philosophy, the Renaissance added Plato and various ancient Neoplatonists to the Aristotle of the medieval universities. More important, perhaps, it began to read late-classical moral philosophies—notably Stoicism and Epicureanism—whose frequent references to the gods made them in effect lost religions. Sometimes inspiring, sometimes scandalous, these recovered moral philosophies introduced personality and inner complexity into the inherited category of paganism. Philosophical recoveries of this sort could remain a purely academic exercise, but for that very reason their influence might be more subtly pervasive. Often, those who studied these texts professed to be seeking only their pro forma subordination to the truth of Roman Catholic Christianity. Nonetheless, the ideas found their way into circulation. To be sure, the few who took the further step of propagating pagan worldviews as actual alternatives to Christian faith or Aristotelian cosmology could pay a high price. The wildly speculative Neoplatonist Giordano Bruno (1548–1600) was burned at the stake as a heretic. But others, scarcely less speculative, spread their ideas with little official interference and in response to widespread popular curiosity.

Comparative Christianity in the Protestant Reformation

Important as the Renaissance was to the development in Europe of a capacity for religious comparison, the Protestant Reformation was surely even more important, for it forced Europeans in one region after another to compare forms of Christianity, accept one, and reject the others. Frequently, this lacerating but formative experience required those who had rejected Catholicism to reject one or more contending forms of

Protestantism as well. This was clearly the case during the English Civil War (1642–51), which forced English Christians to side either with the Anglican king or with the Puritan rebels who beheaded him; but there were other such choices, some of them much more complicated.

Tentative moves toward tolerance during these struggles were far less frequent than fierce mutual persecution and, on either side, the celebration of victims as martyrs. The Catholics tried to dismiss and suppress the Protestants as merely the latest crop of Christian heretics. The Protestants commonly mythologized Rome as Babylon and compared Catholics to the ancient Babylonians, viewing them as pagans who had taken the New Israel, the Christian church, into exile and captivity. The century and a half of the Reformations and the Wars of Religion certainly did not seem to promise a future of sympathetic, mutually respectful religious comparison. And yet within the religious game of impassioned mutual rejection then being played, each side did develop formidable knowledge of the practices, beliefs, and arguments of the other. To the extent that the broader religious comparison initiated during the Enlightenment of the late seventeenth and the eighteenth centuries called for close observation, firsthand testimony, logical analysis, and preparatory study of all kinds, its debt to both the Protestant Reformation and the Catholic Counter-Reformation is enormous.

Particularly important was the historical awareness that the Protestant Reformation introduced into Christian thought. Protestantism took the New Testament to be a historically reliable presentation of earliest Christianity and, using that presentation as a criterion, proceeded to reject the many aspects of Roman Catholic practice that appeared to deviate from it. To be sure, the Roman church had been reading, copying, and devotedly commenting on the Bible for centuries, but it had not been reading it as history. Here the Renaissance paved the way for the Reformation, for the Bible that Rome read was the Bible in a Latin translation; and the Renaissance, as it recovered the knowledge of Hebrew and Greek, had recovered the ability to read the original texts from which that Latin translation had been made. In 1516, the Dutch humanist Deside-rius Erasmus published a bilingual, Greek-Latin edition of the New Testament, correcting the received Latin to bring it into conformity with the newly recovered Greek. Armed with this new tool, the many educated Europeans who knew Latin but not Greek could immediately see that the Latin on which the church had relied for a thousand years was at many points unreliable and in need of revision. In this way, Erasmus, a child of the Renaissance, took a first, fateful step toward historicizing the Bible.

The Reformation, launched just a year later with the publication by Martin Luther of "Ninety-Five Theses on the Power and Efficacy of Indulgences," would take the further, explosive step of historicizing the church itself. To quote a famous line from Reformation polemics, Erasmus "laid the egg that Luther hatched." Thus, two epoch-making historical tools of Protestantism as it would dynamically take shape became integral parts of the later comparative study of non-Christian religions as undertaken by Christian scholars: first, the reconstruction of the composition history of the original texts themselves by scholars who had mastered the original languages; and second, the comparison of later religious practice to earlier through the study of the recovered and historically framed original texts.

In one regard, finally, Protestantism may have indirectly contributed to the comparative study of religion by setting in motion a gradual subversion of the very understanding of religion as a domain separate from ethnicity and culture that had been constitutive of Christian self-understanding almost from its start. Mark C. Taylor argues brilliantly in *After God* (2007) that what is often termed the disappearance of God or the disappearance of the sacred in modernity is actually the integration of that aspect of human experience with the rest of modern experience—a process whose onset he traces to Martin Luther's and John Calvin's sanctification of all aspects of human life as against medieval Christianity's division of the religious life of monks and nuns from the worldly (secular) life of laypeople.[16]

This progressive modern fusion of once separate domains would explain the spread in the West of experiences like that evoked in Todd Boss's "It Is Enough to Enter"—namely, the experience of the holy in ostensibly secular contexts and of the aesthetic in ostensibly religious contexts. Clearly the earlier Christian sense of religion as a separate domain has lingered powerfully in the West. Yet if Taylor is right, then post-Protestant religious modernity in the West, though deeply marked by Protestantism, may be a paradoxical correction of Christianity to the world norm. Or, to put the matter more modestly, the diffuse post-Christian religiosity of the modern West may bear a provocative similarity to the much older but equally diffuse religiosity of South and East Asia.[17]

Toleration, Science, Exploration, and the Need for a New Map

After decades of controversy climaxing in all-out war, it became clear to exhausted Protestants and Catholics alike that neither could dictate the religious future of Europe. The Wars of Religion came to a close in 1648 with the Peace of Westphalia, which, though it by no means established individual freedom of religion, did end international religious war in Europe. Its key principle—*Cuius regio, eius religio* (literally, "Whose the rule, his the religion")—allowed the king or the government of each nation to establish a national religion, but effectively banned any one nation from attempting to impose its religion upon another. At the international level, in other words, there was agreement to disagree. Christian religious fervor itself—at least of the sort that had burned heretics, launched crusades, and so recently plunged Europe into civil war—fell into relative disrepute. The latter half of the seventeenth century saw what Herbert Butterfield (1900–1979), a major historian of Christianity in European history, once called "the Great Secularization."[18]

The old religious allegiances remained, but by slow degrees they began to matter less, even as national allegiance and national devotion— patriotism, as it came to be called—began to take on the moral gravity and ceremonial solemnity of religious commitment and the fallen soldier began to supplant the martyr. In 1689, John Locke published *A Letter Concerning Toleration*, in which he advanced the idea that a state would better guarantee peace within its borders by allowing many religions to flourish than by imposing any one of them. Locke favored a division of the affairs of religion as essentially private from the affairs of state as essentially public, capturing an attitudinal shift

that was already in the air during the Enlightenment and would significantly mark the comparative study of religion as it took lastingly influential
shape in the following century.

More intensely than by nascent toleration, the
mood of the late seventeenth century was marked
by wonder at the discoveries of natural science,
above all those of Isaac Newton, whose major work
establishing the laws of motion and universal grav-
itation was published in 1687. The poet Alexander
Pope captured the popular mood in a famous cou-
plet, written as Newton's epitaph (1730): "Nature,
and Nature's Laws lay hid in Night. / God said, *Let
Newton be!* and All was *Light.*" Light was the master image of the Enlightenment—light, light, and
"more light" (the legendary last words of Johann
Wolfgang von Goethe [1749–1832]). Though the
notion of natural law did not begin with Newton,
his vision of the vast, calm, orderly, and implicitly
benign operation of the laws of motion and gravity
was unprecedented and gave new impetus to the
search for comparable natural laws governing many
other phenomena, including religion. Was there
such a thing as a natural religion? If so, how did
Christianity or any other actual religion relate to

it? This idea, too, was pregnant with the promise of a future comparative study of religion.

While northern European Christianity was fighting the Wars of Religion, southern European Christianity had been transforming both the demography of Christendom and its understanding of the physical geography of the planet. The globe-spanning Portuguese and Spanish empires came into existence with speed comparable only to the Arab conquests of the seventh and eighth centuries. In evangelizing the Americas, the Portuguese and the Spaniards may have made Christianity for the first time the world's largest religion. In any case, their success in establishing colonial trading outposts along the African, Indian, Japanese, and Chinese coasts as well as founding the major Spanish colony of the Philippine Islands (named for the king of Spain) meant that European trade with India and China, above all the lucrative spice trade, no longer needed to pass through Muslim Central Asia or the Muslim Middle East.

Catholic missionaries did not have the success in Asia that they enjoyed in the Americas, yet the highly educated and culturally sophisticated Jesuit missionaries to Asia and the Americas became a significant factor in the evolving religious self-understanding of Europe itself. As extensive missionary reports on the religions of Mexico, Peru, and above all India, China, and Japan reached Europe, they were published and read by many others besides the religious superiors for whom they had been written. Portugal and Spain had opened Europe's doors to a vastly enlarged world. The centuries-old quadripartite European division of the world's religions—Christianity, Judaism, Islam, and Paganism—was still generally in place in European minds. But from that point forward, as the sophistication of the religions of Asia and the Americas as well as the material and social brilliance of their civilizations came into focus, the inadequacy of *paganism* as a catchall term became evident, as did the need for new ways to speak of the newly recognized reality.

A New Reference Book Defines a New Field of Study

If any one occasion can be singled out as the juncture when all these factors coalesced and produced a powerful new engagement with *world religions* in a way that approached the modern understanding of that phrase, it may be the publication in Amsterdam between 1723 and 1737 of an epochal reference work, one that might indeed be seen as a direct ancestor of *The Norton Anthology of World Religions*. Appearing in seven sumptuous volumes comprising more than 3,000 pages with 250 pages of engravings, this encyclopedic production was *Religious Ceremonies and Customs of All the Peoples of the World* (*Cérémonies et coutumes religieuses de tous les peuples du monde*) by Jean Frederic Bernard and Bernard Picart. Here, for the first time, was a presentation in one large work of all the religions of the world then known to Europe. Here, for the first time, was an attempt to reckon with how Europe's religious self-understanding would have to change in light of the previous two centuries of exploration, far-flung evangelization, and colonization.

It is important to note that this work, which was an immediate success and went through many editions and translations (and plagiarizations and piracies) over the next two hundred years, did not begin in the academic world and spread outward to the general public. Its address was directly to the general literate public—to the French public first, but quickly to other publics reading other languages. Jean Frederic Bernard, brilliant but far from famous, was not just its behind-the-scenes research director, editor, and author: he was also its entrepreneurial publisher. It was a masterstroke on his part to secure the collaboration of Bernard Picart, already famous as an engraver producing reproductions of masterpiece paintings in an era before public art museums and long before photography, when what the public knew about art was limited to what they saw in church or what they acquired as engravings. By enabling the European public to see Picart's stunning depictions of Aztec and Asian temples, costumes, and ceremonies, reconstructed from missionaries' descriptions, Bernard and Picart introduced the stimulating possibility of visual comparison. Where visual comparison led, philosophical and other critical comparison were intended to follow—and did.

As noted above, in the latter decades of the seventeenth century and the first of the eighteenth John Locke and a few other thinkers began to argue forcefully for religious toleration. Like Locke, Bernard and Picart were radical Calvinists as well as early "freethinkers," and the Netherlands was unique in their lifetimes as a haven for refugee dissidents and minorities of various kinds. Locke himself took refuge in the Netherlands during a turbulent and threatening period in England. Bernard's Huguenot (French Calvinist) family had fled to the Netherlands when Jean Frederic was a boy. Picart, having abandoned Catholicism, moved there permanently as an adult, joining a large émigré French or French-speaking population in Amsterdam. The Peace of Westphalia, though it had imposed mutual forbearance in religious matters at the international level, had by no means done so at the national level. Protestants were still severely persecuted in France, as were Catholics in England. In the Netherlands, by contrast, though Calvinists were overwhelmingly dominant in public life, the private practice of Catholicism was indulged, while Jews were allowed public worship, and even deists or atheists had little to fear from the government. So it happened that though their great work was written in French, Bernard and Picart had good reason to publish it in the Netherlands.

In their magisterial account of the making of this work, *The Book That Changed Europe: Picart and Bernard's "Religious Ceremonies of the World,"* the historians Lynn Hunt, Margaret C. Jacob, and Wijnand Mijnhardt speculate about another possible consequence of its publication in the Netherlands—namely, the relative oblivion that overtook it in the twentieth century. The most populous European nations have tended to understand the intellectual history of the West first through the minds of their own most influential thinkers, then through those of their major rivals, and only then through authors, however important, whose works were written or published in the smaller nations. Be that as it may, "Picart," as the work was commonly called, had two lasting effects far beyond the borders of the Netherlands. First, by discussing and illustrating the religions of Asia and of the Americas at length, it ended forever the quadripartite division of the world's religions that had structured European thought for eight hundred years. Second, it further solidified the conception of religion as a domain separable from culture and ethnicity. To quote *The Book That Changed Europe*, "This global survey of religious practices effectively *disaggregated and delimited* the sacred, making it specific to time, place, and institutions."[19]

There was now a greatly enlarged universe of religions to reckon with, to be sure, and Christian "teach ye all nations" missionary universalism had already mobilized to engage it. But also now, more strongly than ever, there was "religion" as a proto-sociological category capable of expansion: it had lately been expanded by several new members and conceivably could be expanded further as further reports came in. The universalism of this emergent understanding of religion explains in part why the French Revolution, at the end of the eighteenth century, could presume to declare the "Rights of Man" rather than merely "of the [French] Citizen."

Bernard's and Picart's personal libraries suggest two favorite areas of reading: the ancient classics and travel books. The three historians note that 456 travel books were published in Europe in the fifteenth century, 1,566 in the seventeenth, and 3,540 in the eighteenth.[20] The cocreators' reading in the classics put them in touch with that pluralism of the mind made possible by the Renaissance recovery of classical moral philosophy and by the humanists' imaginative participation in the beliefs that figure so largely in classical literature. Their avid reading of travel reports gave them the enlarged geographical awareness made possible by the age of exploration.

As an early theorist of religion in this transformed mise-en-scène, Bernard blended elements of deist "natural religion" with classic Protestantism. His discussion of the religious customs of the world was scholastically Protestant in its combination of meticulous footnotes and sometimes-strenuous argumentation. More important for its later influence, Bernard's discussion was structurally Protestant in that it cast contemporary religious practice, wherever it was observed around the world, as the corruption of an earlier purity. But where sixteenth-century Protestantism had seen the purity of primitive Christianity, Bernard, writing in the full flush of eighteenth-century enthusiasm for natural science, saw the purity of an early, universal, natural, and "true" religion corrupted by all of the variously scheming priests of the religions reviewed. Despite this structural Calvinism in their philosophy of religion, Bernard and Picard were indebted to John Locke as well as to John Calvin; and especially when the non-Christian religions were under discussion, their manner was more often expository than forensic.

There is no doubt that Bernard discusses and Picart illustrates the religious customs and ceremonies of the world on the assumption both that each religion is, like Christianity, a separate, practice-defined domain and that these domains are all comparable. For better and for worse, the two of them contributed massively to the establishment of "religion" as a category projecting elements of Christian identity upon the vast, newly discovered worlds that lay beyond Christendom. Discussing Bernard and Picart's treatment of indigenous American religion, Hunt, Jacobs, and Mijnhardt declare:

> In short, Picart's images, especially when read alongside Bernard's text, *essentially created the category "religion."* Whereas the text sometimes wandered off on tangents about the sources of particular ceremonies, the similarities between rituals across space (Jewish and Catholic) and time (Roman antiquity and American Indian), or the disputes between scholars on the origins of different peoples, the images kept the focus on the most commonly found religious ceremonies—birth, marriage, death rituals, and grand processions—or on the most strikingly different practices, which

could range from the arcane procedures for the election of popes in Rome to human sacrifice in Mexico. Implicitly, the images transformed religion from a question of truth revealed to a select few of God's peoples (the Jews, the Catholics, and then the Protestants) to an issue of comparative social practices.[21]

The charge of Christian projection can plausibly be lodged against Picart and Bernard's interpretation of particular non-Christian rituals through their nearest equivalents in Christianity or Western antiquity. And yet if such habits of mind were limiting, they were scarcely crippling; and for Picart and Bernard themselves, they were evidently enabling and energizing. Is it true to say that between them, these two "essentially created the category 'religion'"? If they did so, we would claim, they did so largely through the convergence in their work and in themselves of the complex heritage that we have tried to sketch above.

Picart and Bernard carry forward the age-old, often suppressed, but never entirely forgotten understanding of the church as a thing in itself, not to be confounded with any nation or any set of cultural habits or practices. They carry forward the relatively subversive late medieval assumption that philosophy provides a neutral standpoint from which all religions may be compared. When considering religions remote from them in space rather than in time, they carry forward the Renaissance habit of drawing freely on classical paganism interpreted with textual sophistication and literary sympathy. They collate, as no one before them had yet done, the reports streaming into Europe about the religions of Asia and the Americas and, in their most brilliant stroke, they make these the basis for a major artistic effort to *see* what had been reported. They apply to their undertaking a distinct blend of moral seriousness, commercial enterprise, and erudite documentary attention to the particulars of religious practice that is their legacy from French Calvinist Protestantism. Finally, as sons of the Enlightenment, they bring a pioneering openness and breadth of vision to what they study.

Bernard can seem genuinely and intentionally prophetic when he writes:

All religions resemble each other in something. It is this resemblance that encourages minds of a certain boldness to risk the establishment of a project of universal syncretism. How beautiful it would be to arrive at that point and to be able to make people with an overly opinionated character understand that with the help of charity one finds everywhere *brothers*.[22]

The place of good will—the sheer *novelty* of good will—in the study of religion has received far less attention than it deserves. Bernard's dream may seem commonplace now, when courteous interfaith dialogue is familiar enough in much of the West, but it was far from commonplace when he dreamed it.

Like *The Norton Anthology of World Religions*, Bernard and Picart's great work attended first and foremost to rituals and practices, considering beliefs only as expressed or embedded in these. Their work was pathbreaking not just as a summary of what was then known about the religions of the world but also as an early demonstration of what sympathetic, participative imagination would later attain in the study of religion.

In painting their portraits of the religions of the world and in dreaming Bernard's dream ("How beautiful it would be . . . !"), Bernard and Picart were at the same time painting their own intellectual self-portrait as representative Europeans—neither clerics nor philosophers but thoughtful professionals—avid to engage in the comparison of the religions of the world on the widest possible scale. Religious comparison did not begin with them, nor had they personally created the intellectual climate in Europe that welcomed religious comparison once they so grandly attempted it. But it is not too much to say that in their day and to some significant degree because of them, Christian Europe finally learned how to compare religions.

BROADENING THE FOUNDATION, RAISING THE ROOF:
1737–1893

—

In 1737, when Picart and Bernard completed their work, Europe had barely discovered Australia. The peoples of the Arctic and of Oceania were living in nearly unbroken isolation. And even among peoples well known to Europe, Japan was a forbidden kingdom, while China's first engagement with the West had only recently come to a xenophobic close. India was becoming relatively familiar, yet the doors of many smaller nations or regions remained barred. Europe had not yet lost its North and South American colonies to revolution; its later, nineteenth-century colonialist "scramble for Africa" had not yet begun. Russia had not yet expanded eastward to the Pacific. The English colonies in North America had not yet become the

United States or expanded westward to the Pacific. The enlarged world that Bernard and Picart had sought to encapsulate in their illustrated reference work had many enlargements ahead, with corresponding consequences for the study of religion.

Though the intellectual framework for a global and comparative study of religion was essentially in place among an intellectual elite in Europe by the middle of the eighteenth century, much of even the known religious world remained culturally unexplored because the local languages were not understood. The accepted chronology within which Europeans situated new cultural and religious discoveries did not extend to any point earlier than the earliest events spoken of in the Old Testament. All this was to change during the century and a half that separates the publication of Picart from the convocation of the first World's Parliament of Religions at the 1893 Columbian Exposition in Chicago. That date may serve to mark the entrance of the United States of America into the story we have been telling and will bring us to the more immediate antecedents of *The Norton Anthology of World Religions*.

Broadening the Textual Base

Of special relevance for the work of anthologists is the enormous broadening of the textual foundation for religious studies that occurred during this long period. To review that transformation, we will consider the pivotal roles played by four European linguistic prodigies: F. Max Müller (1823–1900), James Legge (1815–1897), Sir William Jones (1746–1794), and Eugène Burnouf (1801–1852). One may grasp at a glance the scope of the documentary change that took place during the 150 years that followed the publication of Bernard and Picart's *Religious Ceremonies and Customs of All the Peoples of the World* by looking forward to the London publication between 1879 and 1910 of *The Sacred Books of the East* in no fewer than fifty volumes.

This enormous reference work, a superlative and in some regards still unsurpassed academic achievement, was produced under the general editorship of F. Max Müller, a German expatriate long resident in England. Müller's role in the nineteenth-century evolution of the disciplines of both comparative linguistics and comparative religious studies is large, but for the moment what concerns us is the sheer scope of the landmark reference work that he edited: two dozen volumes on Hinduism and Jainism translated into English from Sanskrit; nine on Buddhism alike from Sanskrit, from Pali (the canonical language of Indian Buddhism), and from other Asian languages; seven from Chinese on Confucianism, Daoism, and Chinese Buddhism; eight from Persian on Zoroastrianism; and two from Arabic on Islam. The range is astonishing, given that at the time when Bernard and Picart were writing and engraving, knowledge of *any* of these languages, even Arabic, was rare to nonexistent in Europe. How did Europeans learn them over the intervening century and a half? What motivated them to do so? The story blends missionary daring, commercial ambition, and sheer linguistic prowess in different proportions at different times.

Let us begin with Chinese. The first two modern Europeans known to have mastered Chinese were the Italian Jesuit missionaries Michele Ruggieri (1543–1607) and the preternaturally gifted Matteo Ricci (1552–1610), who entered China from the Portuguese island colony of Macao. Over time, as French Jesuits largely succeeded their Italian brethren in the Jesuit mission to China, the reports that they sent back to France about Qing dynasty (1644–1912) culture and the Confucian scholars they encountered stimulated French and broader European curiosity both about China itself and about the Chinese language.[23] Though the Vatican terminated the Jesuits' Chinese mission on doctrinal grounds and though the Qing dynasty suppressed further Christian missionary work and expelled the missionaries themselves in 1724, a seed had been planted. In retirement on Macao, the French Jesuit Joseph Henri Marie de Prémare would compose the West's first-ever Chinese grammar in 1729. Later, during the nineteenth century, as Britain forced a weakening Qing dynasty to sign a treaty establishing coastal enclaves or "treaty ports" under British control, British Protestants commenced a new round of missionary activity in China, including the first attempt to translate the Bible into Chinese.

James Legge, originally a Scottish missionary to China, building on de Prémare's grammar and working with the help of Chinese Christians, undertook a major effort to translate the principal Confucian, Daoist, and Chinese Buddhist classics into English, always with the ultimate intention of promoting Christianity. Meanwhile, in 1814, Europe's first chair of Chinese and Manchu was established at the Collège de France. In 1822, Jean-Pierre Abel-Rémusat published in France a formal grammar of Chinese intended not for missionaries alone but for all interested European students. Legge himself became Oxford University's first professor of Chinese in 1876, and near the end of his life he was F. Max Müller's principal collaborator for Chinese texts in *The Sacred Books of the East.*

European penetration into China proceeded almost entirely from offshore islands or coastal enclaves under European colonial control; China as a whole never became a Western colony. India, by contrast, did indeed become a Western colony—specifically, a British colony—and the West's acquisition of the Indian languages and first encounter with the Indian religious classics is largely a British story. From the sixteenth through the early eighteenth century, Portuguese, Dutch, French, and British commercial interests vied for primacy in the lucrative Indian market. By late in the eighteenth century, however, Britain had overtaken all European rivals and established

India, including what is now Pakistan, as its most important future colony—more lucrative at the time than the thirteen North American colonies that would become the United States of America. Britain's colonial motives were originally mercenary rather than either evangelical or academic, but after British commercial and political control was firmly established in the Indian subcontinent, first cultural and linguistic explorations and then Christian missionary activity would follow.

In the launch of Sanskrit studies in the West, no figure looms larger than Sir William Jones, an Anglo-Welsh jurist in Calcutta who was as prodigiously gifted in language study as Matteo Ricci or James Legge. Fascinated by all things Indian, Jones founded an organization, the Asiatic Society, to foster Indian studies; and in 1786, on its third anniversary, he delivered a historic lecture on the history of language itself. In it, he expounded the thesis that Sanskrit, Greek, Latin, most of the European vernacular languages, and probably Persian were all descendants of a vanished common ancestor. Today, linguistic scholarship takes for granted the reality of "Proto-Indo-European" as a lost ancient language whose existence is the only conceivable explanation for the similarities that Jones may not have been the very first to chart but was certainly the first to bring to a large European public.

Jones's lecture detonated an explosion of European interest in studying Sanskrit and in tracing the family tree of the Indo-European, or "Aryan," languages, including all the languages mentioned in the previous paragraph but notably excluding Hebrew and Arabic—descendants of a different linguistic ancestor, later postulated as Proto-Semitic. (In the Bible, it is from Noah's son Shem—*Sēm* in Greek—that the peoples of the Middle East are descended—whence the term *Sem*-itic.) Now, the New Testament had been written in Greek rather than Hebrew or Aramaic, and Western Christianity had quickly left its Aramaic-speaking Palestinian antecedents behind and become a Greek-speaking Mediterranean religion. Did that mean that Christianity was actually Indo-European, or "Aryan," rather than Semitic, even though Jesus and Paul were Jews? This became one cultural strand within the European enthusiasm for Sanskrit studies, as further discussed below. Suffice it to say for now that it was during this period that *Semitic* and *Semitism* were coined as linguistic terms and the anti-Jewish *anti-Semitic* and *anti-Semitism* were coined as prejudicial, pseudo-anthropological counterterms.

Of greater immediate importance for the broadening of the study of religion was the window that Sanskrit opened on an almost unimaginably vast Indian literature whose most ancient and venerated texts, the Vedas, may be as old as, or even older than, the oldest strata of the Old Testament. Sanskrit is the classical language of India, no longer spoken and perhaps artificially perfected as a sacred language at some unrecoverable point in the past. But India has in addition a great many vernacular languages, more of them than Europe has, and in a number of these languages, other extensive Hindu literatures exist. These, too, gradually came to light in the nineteenth and the early twentieth centuries as knowledge of the relevant languages gradually spread to Europe.

India, for all its immense internal variety, did and does have a sense of itself as a single great place and of its gods as the gods of that place. Siddhartha Gautama, the Buddha, was born in India, and Indian Buddhism was the first Buddhism. Buddhist texts in Sanskrit are foundational for all students of Buddhism. But after some centuries had passed, Buddhism largely died out in India, living on in Sri Lanka, Southeast Asia, China, Korea, Japan, Mongolia, and Tibet. The linguistic and cultural variety of these countries was enormous. The Buddha was not called by the same name in all of them (in China, for example, he was called "Fo"). Western travelers, not knowing the languages of any of the countries where Buddhism was dominant, were slow to recognize even such basic facts as that the Buddha himself was a historical personage and not simply one among the many deities and demons whose statues they saw in their travels.

Donald S. Lopez, Jr., Buddhism editor for *The Norton Anthology of World Religions*, has written or edited several books telling the fascinating tale of how the puzzle of international Buddhism slowly yielded to the painstaking Western acquisition of several difficult languages and the related gradual recovery of a second, astoundingly large multilingual religious literature standing alongside that of Hinduism. In his *From Stone to Flesh: A Short History of the Buddha* (2013), Lopez allows what we might call the statue story—the gradual realization that sculptures of the Buddha represented a man, not a god—to become the human face on this much larger and less visible story of literary and historical recovery.[24]

In the story of how a broad textual foundation was laid for the study of Buddhism, a third linguistic genius stands between the Anglo-Welsh William Jones and the expatriate German F. Max Müller—namely, the French polymath Eugène Burnouf, the last of the four gifted linguists mentioned near the start of this section. Because of the enthusiasm for Sanskrit studies that Jones had touched off in Europe, copies of texts in Sanskrit began reaching European "orientalists" during the first decades of the nineteenth century. Those that arrived from India itself, as they were translated, would enable the assembly of the twenty-one volumes of Hindu texts that open Müller's *Sacred Books of the East*. Initially, however, no Sanskrit texts dealing with Buddhism were forthcoming from the Indian subcontinent. This situation would change, thanks to the fortuitous posting of an energetic and culturally alert English officer, Brian Houghton Hodgson (1801?–1894), to Nepal, where Buddhism thrived. Hodgson collected dozens of

Nepalese Buddhist texts in Sanskrit, including the crucially important *Lotus Sutra*, and arranged for copies to be shipped to Europe.

Burnouf had been appointed to the Sanskrit chair at the Collège de France five years before the first shipment from Hodgson arrived. Thanks in part to earlier work he had done in the study of Pali, the Indian language in which the oldest Buddhist texts survive, Burnouf seems to have quickly grasped that what he had before him was the key to the historical roots of Buddhism in India. But this recognition was father to the further insight that Buddhism was the first true world religion (or, as he was inclined to think, the first internationally embraced moral philosophy) in human history. Burnouf was among the first, if not the very first, to see Buddhism whole. His 1844 *Introduction à l'histoire du Buddhisme indien* (*Introduction to the History of Indian Buddhism*) was the first of a projected four volumes that, had he lived to write them, would surely have been his greatest work. The one lengthy volume that he did bring to completion was already of epoch-making importance, particularly in light of his influence on his student F. Max Müller.

What the discovery and European importa-
tion of the classical religious literatures of India
and China meant for the comparative study of religion in the West can be signaled concisely in the
terms *Confucianism*, *Daoism* (earlier, *Taoism*), *Hinduism*, and *Buddhism*. They are all Western coinages,
hybrids combining an Asian word at the front end
and the Greek morpheme *–ism* at the back end,
and each represents the abstraction of a separate
domain of religious literature and religious practice from the cultural and ethnic contexts in which
it originated. The coinage of these terms themselves may not coincide exactly with the recovery
of the respective literatures; but to the extent that
nineteenth-century Western scholarship viewed
the texts as the East's equivalent of the Bible, it
all but unavoidably engaged them on structurally
Christian and even Protestant terms, thereby fur-
thering the European conception of each related
–ism as a religion in Europe's now consolidated and
universalist sense of the word.

Structurally, Protestant influence was apparent
again whenever, in the manner of Bernard and
Picart, the great nineteenth-century linguist-
historians judged the earlier texts to be superior

to the later ones. Thus, in the interpretation of newly available Chinese texts, the earlier, more interior or "philosophical" versions of Daoism and Confucianism were often judged superior to the later, more ceremonial or "religious" versions, in which Laozi or Kongzi (Confucius) seemed to be deified or quasi-deified. Similarly, in the nineteenth-century interpretation of Hindu literature, India's British colonial rulers celebrated the supposed nobility and purity of the early Vedas and Upanishads while disparaging later Hindu religious texts and especially actual nineteenth-century Hindu practice. In the Buddhist instance, Eugène Burnouf set the early, human, historical Indian Buddha—whom he understood to have preached an ethics of simplicity and compassion—against the later, superhuman metaphysical Buddha. Consciously or unconsciously, Burnouf's contrast of the historical and the metaphysical Buddha coincided strikingly with the contrast then being drawn for a wide European audience between the historical Jesus of Nazareth and the divine Christ, the God incarnate of Christian faith.

In short, as this new, broadened textual foundation was laid for the documentary study of Hinduism, Buddhism, and Daoism, a Christian theology of scripture and a post-Protestant philosophy of history were often projected upon it by the brilliant but Eurocentric scholars who were shaping the field. However, once primary texts are in hand, their intrinsic power can exert itself against any given school of interpretation. Thus, for example, late twentieth-century scholarship began to foreground and valorize the late and the popular over the early and the elite in several traditions, dignifying colorful texts and demotic practices once thought unworthy of serious scholarly attention.

Though nineteenth-century scholars might shudder at such a shift, it is essentially to them that we owe the availability of the key texts themselves. To be sure, the full recovery and the translation of these literatures are works in progress; nonetheless, knowledge of their great antiquity and their scope—barely even dreamed of by Picart and Bernard—was substantially complete by the end of the nineteenth century. The literary foundation had been put in place for an enormously enlarged effort at comparative study.

Enlarging the Chronological Frame

As already noted, Europeans as late as the early nineteenth century situated new cultural and religious discoveries, including all the texts whose recovery we have been discussing, in a chronology of religion understood to commence no earlier than the earliest events spoken of in the Old Testament. This framework led to efforts, comical in retrospect, to link newly discovered places and newly encountered legends or historical memories in Asia and the Americas to place-names in the book of Genesis, to the Noah story of Genesis 6–9, and to legends about the eastward travels of the apostles of Christ. All this would change with a discovery that might be described as blowing the roof off recorded history.

During Napoleon Bonaparte's occupation of Egypt in 1798–99, a French soldier stationed near the town of Rosetta in the Nile delta discovered a large stone bearing an inscription in three scripts: first, ancient Egyptian hieroglyphics, a script that no one then could read; second, another unknown script, which turned out to represent a later form of the Egyptian language; and finally, a third script, Greek. It took two decades of work, but in 1822, Jean-François Champollion deciphered this "Rosetta Stone." In the ensuing decades, his breakthrough enabled later scholars to translate hundreds of ancient Egyptian hieroglyphic inscriptions recovered from the ruins of ancient Egypt's immense tombs and temples and to discover, as they did so, that the Egyptians had maintained a remarkably complete chronology stretching back millennia before the oldest historical events recorded in the Bible. Decades of archaeological excavation in Egypt further enabled the construction of a chronological typology of Egyptian pottery. And then, since Egyptian pottery and pottery fragments are found all over the ancient Near East in mounds (tells) left by the repeated destruction and reconstruction of cities on the same sites, Egyptian pottery could be used to date sites far removed from Egypt. Over time, the Egyptian chronology would become the anchor for a chronological reconstruction of the entire lost history of the Near East, much of it written on thousands of archaeologically recovered clay tablets inscribed in the Mesopotamian cuneiform script that at the start of the eighteenth century was as undecipherable as Egyptian hieroglyphic.

The cuneiform (literally, "wedge-shaped") writing system was used as early as the late fourth millennium B.C.E. for the representation of Sumerian, a mysterious language without known antecedents or descendants. Sumeria, the oldest civilization of the ancient Near East—situated near the southern tip of Iraq, just north of the Persian Gulf—appears to have invented cuneiform writing. Most extant cuneiform texts, however, survive as small tablets representing several other ancient languages, all of them Semitic, rather than Sumerian. Starting in the mid-nineteenth century, hundreds of thousands of cuneiform tablets were recovered by archaeological excavations nearly as important as those in Egypt.

Cuneiform was deciphered thanks to the discovery in Persia in 1835 of a trilingual set of incised cuneiform wall inscriptions in Behistun (Bisitun, Iran) that, like the Rosetta Stone, included one already-known language—in this case ancient Persian—that scholars were eventually able to recognize behind the mysterious script. The challenge lay in going beyond the Persian of that inscription to decipher the language—now known to be the Mesopotamian Semitic language Akkadian—represented by one of the other two inscriptions. Though Eugène Burnouf played almost as important a role in this decipherment as he played in the recovery of Indian Buddhism, it is Henry Rawlinson, the British East India Company officer who first visited the Behistun inscriptions in 1835, whose name is usually linked to the recovery for European scholarship of the lost cuneiform literatures of Mesopotamia.

None of the now-extinct religions whose literatures survive in cuneiform is anthologized in *The Norton Anthology of World Religions*; the editors agreed to anthologize only major, living international religions. But the recovery of these lost literatures significantly affected the evolving historical context for all religious comparison. What these texts made clear was that recorded history had not dawned in Athens and Jerusalem. The religion of ancient Israel, in particular, was relocated from the dawn of history to a late morning hour, and thus could no longer be seen as in any sense the ancient ancestor of all the religions of the world. On the contrary, it now became possible to study the Bible itself comparatively, as a text contemporaneous with other texts, produced by a religion contemporaneous with and comparable to other ancient Semitic religions. And since the Bible is an anthology produced over a millennium, it became possible and even imperative to study each stratum within the Bible as contemporaneous with differing sets of non-Israelite religions and their respective texts.

European Protestantism, accustomed since the Reformation to employing the Bible as a historically reliable criterion for criticizing and revising the inherited practices of Christianity, was deeply affected by the discovery of both prebiblical and contemporaneous extrabiblical literatures, for they were clearly a way to deepen the historical understanding of the Bible. But the recovery of these literatures, set alongside related evidence from archaeological excavation, was a threat as well as an opportunity. It was an opportunity because it enabled illuminating comparisons of key motifs in Hebrew mythology with their counterparts in other ancient Near Eastern mythologies; it was a threat because though it corroborated the historicity of some biblical events, it undermined that of others.

Religious truth can be conveyed as well through fiction as through history. Patristic and medieval Christianity were content for centuries to search the Bible for moral allegories rather than for historical evidence. Where history was not a central concern, comparative Semitic studies could and did enrich the linguistic and literary interpretation of the Bible without impugning its religious authority. But because Protestantism, rejecting allegorical interpretation, had consistently emphasized and valorized the historical or "plain," non-allegorical content of the Bible, Protestant Christianity had particular trouble entertaining the notion that the Bible could be historically false in some regards and yet still religiously valid. A desire to defend the Old Testament as historically valid thus arose as a second motivation for Semitic studies. In the process, the prestige of the study of history itself as an intellectual discipline able to produce ostensibly authoritative judgments about religion was significantly enhanced if not indeed considerably inflated.

The discovery of the Rosetta Stone and the Behistun inscriptions affected the comparative study of Islam as well, though less directly. The recovery of lost Semitic languages and their lost literatures invited comparative linguistic study of the now-increased number of languages clearly related to Aramaic, Hebrew, and Arabic—the three principal languages of this family that were already known at the end of the eighteenth century. This study led to the postulated existence of a lost linguistic ancestor, Proto-Semitic, from which they were all plausibly descended. Proto-Semitic then began to play a role in the study of the religions practiced by the peoples who spoke these languages, somewhat like the role that Proto-Indo-European was playing in the study of the religions practiced by the peoples who spoke Sanskrit, Greek, Latin, German, and the other languages of that linguistic family.

As Proto-Semitic was reconstructed, moreover, it became clear to scholars that classical Arabic, the Arabic of the Qur'an, resembled it very closely and thus was an extremely ancient language that preserved almost the entire morphology of the lost ancestor of all the Semitic languages. Classical Hebrew, by contrast, was shown to be a much younger Semitic language. In an era of so much speculation about the relationship between ancient religions and ancient languages, the near-identity of classical Arabic and Proto-Semitic suggested to some that Islam might have preserved and carried forward ancient features of a Semitic proto-religion that was the lost ancestor of all the Semitic religions, just as Proto-Semitic was the lost ancestor of all the Semitic languages.

Orientalism, Neo-Hellenism, and the Quest for the Historical Jesus

The emergence of "Semitic languages" and "Semitic religions" as groups whose members were identifiable through comparison meant that biblical studies and Qur'anic studies—or more generally the study of ancient Israel and that of pre- and proto-Islamic Arabia—were more closely linked in the nineteenth century than they usually are in the twenty-first. Julius Wellhausen (1844–1918), a major German biblical scholar, reconstructed the formative stages of both. Historical linguists in Wellhausen's day who engaged in such comparative study of languages and history were called "orientalists." *Orientalism* is a term now associated with cultural condescension to the peoples of a region extending from Turkey through Persia to the borders of Afghanistan; but when first coined, it connoted primarily a stance of neutral comparison across that large cultural realm, a realm that the study of the languages, ancient and modern, had now thrown open for historical study as never before.

Interest in the language and history of classical Greece also grew enormously in nineteenth-century Europe, fed both by Hellenic revivalism and by Christian anxiety. The upper class generally celebrated Greek literature and thought as expressing a humane ideal distinct from and even superior to that of Christianity. In the late eighteenth century, in his *The History of the Decline and Fall of the Roman Empire* (1776–88), the English historian Edward Gibbon had already presented the emergence of Christianity as in itself the key factor in the decline of a superior classical civilization; Gibbon elevated the nobility and civic virtue of republican Rome above the faith, hope, and charity of Pauline Christianity as celebrated by classic Protestantism.

In the nineteenth century, it was Greece rather than Rome that defined the cultural beau ideal for an intellectual elite across western Europe. The German philosopher Friedrich Nietzsche (1844–

1900), a classicist by training, was steeped in this philo-Hellenic tradition and drew heavily upon it for his well-known critique of Christianity. In its devout classicism, nineteenth-century European culture thus continued and intensified a celebration of an idealized and indeed a more or less mythologized Greece that had begun during the Renaissance and continued during the Enlightenment.

This European cultural identification with Greece, whether or not tinged with antipathy toward Christianity, sometimes worked symbiotically with a larger geographical/cultural identification already mentioned—namely, Europe's identification with the larger world of the Indo-European peoples as distinct from and superior to the disparaged Semitic peoples, most notably the Jews. Religiously motivated Christian prejudice against Jews had by no means disappeared, but it was now joined by a form of pseudoscientific racism that made more of national than of religious difference. Because nationalist self-glorification linked to invidious anti-Semitism had a seriously distorting effect on the comparative study of religion in nineteenth-century Europe, the full enfranchisement of Europe's Jews as fellow scholars

would have, as we will see, a comparably important corrective effect.

A second motivation for classical studies, especially in Lutheran Germany, was Christian: an
urgently felt need to write the still-unwritten
history of the New Testament in the context of
first-century Hellenistic Judaism. The historical
reliability of the New Testament had been the foundation of the Lutheran critique of sixteenth-century
Catholicism. But nineteenth-century New Testament scholars now claimed to recognize adultera-
tions by the church within the Gospels themselves.
To exaggerate only slightly, the challenge that
nineteenth-century Protestant scholars saw themselves facing was to recover the historical Jesus from
the church-corrupted Gospels in the same way that
they understood the sixteenth-century reformers to
have recovered the historical practice of Christianity from the corrupted church practice of their day.

"Historical Jesus" scholarship of this sort grew
enormously in scope and erudition during the
first decades of the nineteenth century, fed by the
growing prestige of history as a social science and
climaxing with the publication in 1835–36 of David
Friedrich Strauss's massive, learned, sensationally

successful, but scandalously skeptical *Life of Jesus, Critically Examined*, a German work that appeared in English in 1846 in an anonymous translation by the aspiring English novelist George Eliot (Marian Evans). Decades of further scholarship followed, some of it indirectly stimulated once again by archaeology. As the excavations by Heinrich Schliemann (1822–1890) proved that there was a Troy and that a great war had occurred there, thus allegedly proving the historical reliability of the *Iliad*, so, it was hoped, further archaeological and historical research might yet demonstrate the historical reliability of the New Testament.

A denouement occurred in 1906 with the publication of the German first edition of Albert Schweitzer's epoch-making *The Quest of the Historical Jesus*.[25] Schweitzer believed that the quest for the historical Jesus had actually succeeded as history. Yet the recovered historical Jesus was more a problem for contemporary Christianity than a solution, the renowned scholar ruefully concluded. Schweitzer's work continues to haunt historical Jesus scholarship, even though fresh quests and fresh alleged recoveries of the lost historical Jesus, both learned and popular, have continued to appear.

In sum, narrowly Christian though the quest for the historical Jesus may seem, it did much to establish historical study as the default mode of religious study. Its shadow lies across studies of the historical Buddha, the historical Laozi, and the historical Muhammad, among others, stamping them all with the still rarely challenged assumption that in the study of any religious tradition, historical truth will prove the indisputable and finally the foundational form of truth.

The Haskalah and Its Impact on the Comparative Study of Religion

The character of the literature of religious studies is determined as much by who is writing as by what is written about. So far, we have concentrated on changes in what was available as subject matter to be written about, thanks to the recovery of religious literatures either lost in time or remote in place. We turn now to a new line of inquiry and a new question: Who was to be commissioned to conduct the study, to do the writing, to tell the story of the religions of the world? In the late eighteenth and the nineteenth centuries, above all in

Germany, a Jewish religious, cultural, and intellectual movement called the *Haskalah* emerged, one of whose effects would be the historic enfranchisement of Jews as, for the first time, full participants in Europe's comparative study of religion. Before saying more about the impact of the Haskalah upon secular religious studies in Europe, we should briefly review its direct and complex impact upon the Jews of Europe themselves.

Religiously, thanks in good measure to the pathbreaking work of the Jewish-German philosopher Moses Mendelssohn (1729–1786), the Haskalah gave rise to Reform Judaism as a revised form of Jewish belief and practice more attentive to the Tanakh, or Hebrew Bible (Christianity's Old Testament), than to the Talmud. However uncontroversial it may seem in the twenty-first century for the reformers to honor the biblical prophets rather than the Talmudic sages as the ethical pinnacle of the Jewish tradition, the shift was highly disruptive in the late eighteenth and the nineteenth centuries, for the emphasis in Jewish religious practice until then had been squarely on the Talmud and on the rabbinical sages whose debates, preserved in the Talmud, had made the rabbinate the final authority

in Jewish religious observance. In the rabbinic tradition, the Talmud is the heart of the "Oral Torah"
that Moses, the original rabbi (teacher), received
from God and conveyed in speech to his first (rabbinical) students, beginning a teacher-to-student
chain that legitimated the rabbinate as authoritative. To undercut the Talmud, Rabbinic Judaism's
foundational second scripture, was thus to undercut the rabbis themselves.

Reform Judaism was religiously unsettling in
another way because by going back to the Bible,
thereby setting aside centuries of venerable Jewish tradition and subverting established rabbinical
religious authority, its founders, beginning with
Moses Mendelssohn, delivered a critique that
bore a striking structural resemblance to German Lutheranism's back-to-the-Bible critique
of Roman Catholicism. The Jewish reformation
looked rather like the Christian, to the exhilara-
tion of many Jews at the time in Lutheran northern Germany but to the consternation of others.

Religiously disruptive in these ways, the
Haskalah—often referred to as the Jewish
Enlightenment—represented as well a major
turning point in Jewish European cultural life,

away from oppressive and once inescapable social restriction and confinement. The *Maskilim*, as the leaders of the Haskalah were called, recognized that the dawn of a culture of toleration in Christian Europe might just light the path to an escape for Jews who were willing to acculturate in certain manageable ways. Mendelssohn himself, for example, became an acknowledged master of literary German as written by the intellectual elite of Berlin. German culture was then entering its most brilliant century. In an earlier century, German Jews would have had to become Christians to exit the ghetto and take part. But absent the requirement to convert, perhaps German Jews could become Jewish Germans. Such was the tacit hope of the Haskalah.

As Reform Judaism grew in popularity, thousands of Jews gambled that the ghetto walls were indeed coming down, and ultimately they were not mistaken. Despite the murderous anti-Semitism that would rise in the later nineteenth century and the genocide that would so profoundly scar the twentieth, a page had been turned for good in Western academic life—not least in the comparative study of religion.

The Haskalah mattered in one further, only slightly narrower regard: while no longer deferring to the immense corpus of rabbinic literature as authoritative, the Maskilim did not ignore it. On the contrary, they began to apply to it the same techniques of critical scholarship that the Renaissance had pioneered and that Protestantism and the Enlightenment had further developed for the interpretation of the Bible and other classical texts. The process of critically editing and translating the rabbinic literature, which placed yet another major religious literature within the reach of secular study, began very slowly and approached completion only in the twentieth century. Yet were it not for the Maskilim, that great work would not have been undertaken.

Most important of all, however, was the inclusion of Christianity's original "other" in the corps of those attempting in the West to make comparative sense of the religions of the world. This inclusion was truly a watershed event, for it foreshadowed a long list of subsequent, cumulatively transformative inclusions of the previously excluded. Religious studies in the twenty-first century is open to all qualified participants, but such has not always been the case. Broadening the textual basis for religious studies and exploding the temporal frame around it were important nineteenth-century developments. Broadening the composition of the population that would engage in religious studies was even more important.

The gradual inclusion of non-Christian scholars in the Western discussion of world religions has not entailed retiring the historically Christian but now secularized concept of religion (or the related concept of world religions), but Christian or Western scholars have lost any presumptive right to serve as moderators or hosts of the discussion. The overcoming of insufferable condescension, not to speak of outright prejudice, has played a part, but so too, and more importantly, have matters of perception, perspective, and the "othering" of Christianity: the rest had long been accustomed to see themselves through the eyes of the West; now the West has begun to see itself through the eyes of the rest.

The dynamic entry of Europe's Jews not just into the European study of religion but also into many other areas of European life brought about a massive backlash in the late nineteenth century, then the Nazi genocide in the twentieth, the post–

World War II triumph of Zionism, and belatedly, among other consequences, a distinct mood of remorse and repentance in late twentieth-century European Christianity.[26] Somewhat analogous emotions accompanied the end of European colonialism during the same late twentieth-century decades amid exposés of the exploitation and humiliation suffered by the colonized. The comparative study of religion has both influenced and been influenced by these ongoing revisionist shifts of mood and opinion, but, to repeat, the first steps down this long path were taken by and during the Haskalah.

Evolution and the Comparative Study of Religion

While the decipherment of Egyptian hieroglyphic and Mesopotamian cuneiform were still throwing new light on the earliest centuries of recorded history, Charles Darwin's *On the Origin of Species by Means of Natural Selection* in 1859 and *The Descent of Man, and Selection in Relation to Sex* in 1871 shone a beam into the deeper darkness of the unrecorded, biological prehistory of the human species. At the time, no one, including Darwin, knew just how old *Homo sapiens* was as a species; the technique of absolute dating by the measurement of radioactive decay would not be developed until the mid-twentieth century. What Darwin could already demonstrate from the fossil record, however, was that the human species had evolved from earlier species in a process that antedated recorded history. The implications of this discovery for all forms of scientific and historical investigation were enormous and are still being explored. For the study of religion, the discovery meant that behind the religions of recorded history, there now stood in principle all the religions of human prehistory. At what point in human evolution did religion first appear, or was that even the right question? Should the question rather be about precursors to religion—earlier behaviors that would evolve into what we now call religion? How, if at all, could the practitioners of these prehistoric proto-religions or precursors to religion be studied?

Answers to that question are still being devised, but none involves their texts, for they left none. Tempting as it would be to explore new work being done on the evolution of religion before the invention of writing, such work is not properly a part of the study of religion to which *The Norton Anthology of World Religions* contributes, for it is, after all, a collection of texts. To the best of *our* current (and ever provisional) knowledge, the human species emerged some two hundred thousand years ago in southwest Africa and migrated from there eastward and then northward through the Great Rift Valley in what appear to be two noteworthy spikes. One spike proceeded by way of Lake Victoria up the Nile River to where its delta empties into the Mediterranean Sea. The other spike crossed from Africa to Arabia at the Strait of Bab el Mandeb and then proceeded along the southeast coast of Arabia to the Strait of Hormuz, where it crossed into Asia. From there, one stream of human migrants veered northward to the delta of the Tigris River at the upper end of the Persian Gulf, while the other moved southward to the delta of the Indus River. The Indus delta and the river system above it cradled the civilization that, as it moved south into the Indian subcontinent, would produce the Vedas, written in Sanskrit, the earliest scriptures of ancient India. The Nile and the Tigris deltas and the river systems that lay above them would together define the "Fertile Crescent" within which ancient Israel would produce the earliest Hebrew scriptures. The invention of writing in the Tigris delta (Sumer) and the Nile Valley (Egypt) does not antedate the late fourth millennium B.C.E. The oldest works honored as scripture by Hinduism or by Judaism may be a full millennium younger than that. As recoverable from surviving texts, the story of the world's major, living, international religions can reach no further back in time than this.

To concede this much is not to concede that the earlier, preliterate evolution of religion cannot be recovered at all or indeed even recovered in a way that would link it to the story told here. It is to concede only that any such recovery must rely on archaeological and paleological resources very unlike the historical texts anthologized in *The Norton Anthology of World Religions*.

The First World's Parliament of Religions

We may close this review of the development of religious studies between 1737 and 1893 with a visit to the World's Parliament of Religions at the World's Columbian Exposition in Chicago in 1893. The vast exposition, which ran for six months and attracted millions of visitors, was a celebration of progress—scientific, political, and cultural—during the five hundred years since Columbus had discovered America. (The exposition missed its intended 1892 opening by a few months.) Though the organizers often seemed to tacitly assume that the latest and greatest chapter in world progress was the American chapter and that thriving, optimistic Chicago was the epitome of American progress, nonetheless an exuberant, generally benevolent and inclusive curiosity characterized much on display. And though there was condescension in the presentation of model villages from "primitive" societies as natural history exhibits, there was also an acknowledgment that many fascinating and once entirely unknown societies were now no longer unknown and could be presented for the instruction of the interested.

As for the World's Parliament of Religions, it seemed to reflect a contemporary, enlightened, Protestant American view that there existed—or there could come into existence—something like a generic religion whose truth all specific religions could acknowledge without renouncing their

respective identities. This view may have owed
something to the many translations and plagiarizations of *The Religious Ceremonies and Customs of All
the Peoples of the World* that for a century and a half
had been steadily propagating Bernard and Picart's
confidence that a pure, "natural" religion under-
lay the variously corrupted historical religions of
the world. It may have owed something as well to
the 1890 publication of James Frazer's *The Golden
Bough*, a romantic and enormously popular work
that marshaled classical mythology and selected
early anthropological studies of primitive tribes in a
grand evolutionary march from magic to science.[27]
It may have reflected in addition the gradual influence on American Protestants of the Enlightenment
ideas underpinning the United States Constitution.
Under the Constitution, since there was no "religious test" for public office, a Hindu, a Buddhist,
a Muslim, or even an atheist could legally become
president.[28] The legal leveling explicit in the Constitution implicitly encouraged a comparable leveling in American society, first among Protestants but
later extended to Catholics and Jews, and gradually
to the adherents of other religions. The process was
slow, but its direction was unmistakable.

What is most remarkable about the Parliament, however, is the simple fact that when the organizers invited representatives of Hinduism, Buddhism, Daoism, Confucianism, Shinto, Jainism, Islam, and Zoroastrianism to come together and deliberate with Christians and Jews, everyone accepted the invitation. Swami Vivekananda (1863–1902) accepted both the invitation and the idea behind it—namely, that Hinduism was a world religion. He did not object that there was no such thing as "Hinduism," that the religious life of India was not a separate province within a postulated empire named "religion," that Indians who honored the Vedas did not see themselves as en route to any brighter collective religious future, and so forth and so on. Objections like this are legitimate, but Vivekananda agreed to attend anyway, gave a sensationally well-received speech, and went on to found the Vedanta Society as an American branch of Hinduism. Plainly enough, he had begun to construe Hinduism as potentially a global religion, separable from Indian ethnicity. The Sri Lankan Buddhist Anagarika Dharmapala (1864–1933) did something similar. In the real world of religious practice, these were important ratifying votes for a vision of world religious pluralism.

"How beautiful it would be," Jean Frederic Bernard had written, "to arrive at that point and to be able to make people with an overly opinionated character understand that with the help of charity one finds everywhere *brothers*." If the organizers of the World's Parliament of Religions thought that they had arrived at that blessed point when Swami Vivekananda thrilled his American audience with the opening words of his oration, "Sisters and Brothers of America," they were mistaken. And yet something was happening. A change was taking place. In various related European and American venues, a subtle but distinct shift of attitude was under way.

Is it possible to contemplate beliefs that one does not share and practices in which one does not engage and to recognize in them the shaping of a life that one can recognize as human and even good? When attitudes shift on a question as basic as that one, novelists and poets are often the first to notice. The novelist Marcel Proust wrote as follows about the Hindu and Buddhist concepts of *samsara* and *karma*—though without ever using

those words—in his early twentieth-century masterpiece *In Search of Lost Time* (1913–27):

> He was dead. Dead for ever? Who can say? . . .
> All that we can say is that everything is arranged
> in this life as though we entered it carrying a
> burden of obligations contracted in a former
> life; there is no reason inherent in the conditions
> of life on this earth that can make us consider
> ourselves obliged to do good, to be kind and
> thoughtful, even to be polite, nor for an atheist
> artist to consider himself obliged to begin over
> again a score of times a piece of work the admi-
> ration aroused by which will matter little to his
> worm-eaten body, like the patch of yellow wall
> painted with so much skill and refinement by
> an artist destined to be for ever unknown and
> barely identified under the name Vermeer. All
> these obligations, which have no sanction in our
> present life, seem to belong to a different world,
> a world based on kindness, scrupulousness, self-
> sacrifice, a world entirely different from this one
> and which we leave in order to be born on this
> earth, before perhaps returning there to live
> once again beneath the sway of those unknown

laws which we obeyed because we bore their precepts in our hearts, not knowing whose hand had traced them there[.][29]

Marcel Proust was not a Hindu; he was a Frenchman of Jewish descent. Like not a few writers of his day, he may have been influenced by Frazer's *The Golden Bough*, but *In Search of Lost Time* is in any case a novel, not a work of science, philosophy, or theology. And yet we might say that in the words quoted, Proust is a Hindu by sympathetic, participative imagination and thus among the heirs of Jean Frederic Bernard and Bernard Picart. This kind of imaginatively participant sympathy was taking hold in a new way.

In the United States, the World's Parliament of Religions reflected the same Zeitgeist and heralded, moreover, an organizational change that would occur in the latter third of the following century, building on all that had transpired since Bernard dreamed his dream. That change—the decision of the National Association of Bible Instructors to reincorporate in 1964 as the American Academy of Religion—reflected the emergent conviction that some knowledge of the world's religions was properly a part of every American's education.[30]

If American intellectual culture is distinctive in any regard, it is distinctive in its penchant for popularization or for the democratization of knowledge. The intellectual leadership of the country has generally assumed that the work of intellectual discovery is not complete until everybody has heard the news. But judgment about what constitutes "news"—that is, what subjects constitute the core of education for all people—has changed over time, and knowledge of the world's religions has not always been on the list. It was during the twentieth century that it made the list, and so for the study of religion we may regard the World's Parliament of Religions as opening the twentieth century.

In the comparative study of religion, Europe was America's teacher until the end of World War II. The secular, neutral comparative study of religion was a European inspiration. The heavy lifting necessary to assemble linguistic and archaeological documentary materials for such study—the story we have been reviewing here—was almost entirely a European achievement as well. But a distinctive aspect of the American contribution to the story has been the impulse to share inspirations, achievements, and knowledge gained in the study of religion with the general public. A work like *The Norton Anthology of World Religions*, intended for the college undergraduate or the willing general reader, is a work entirely in the American grain and one that carries this origin story into the twenty-first century.

WHY RELIGION?

As *The Norton Anthology of World Religions* went to press, I was confident as general editor, having read every word in it at least once over the course of the previous nine years, that we had produced a tool that could usefully serve many different purposes, many different agendas. Yet I was aware, too, that when religion is the subject, however academically and dispassionately a scholar may discuss it, readers will ask, "But where are you personally? What is your religion? Are you religious or not?"

These are not scholarly questions, and scholars have every reason to decline them. However, readers also have every reason to ask them and to wonder about the answers when none is forthcoming. The postscript that follows here was a small, personal, and decidedly unscholarly attempt to con-

cede a little something to this legitimate curiosity.
The nature of the subject seemed to me to constitute an argument for a brief and modest bending of
the normal academic rules.

Many years ago, having ceased to practice the
Roman Catholicism of my youth and young adult-
hood without adopting any replacement for it or
resolving much of anything to my own satisfaction,
I happened in a bookstore upon Bertrand Russell's
essay "A Free Man's Worship" (1903), published
with his better-known "Why I Am Not a Christian" (1927) in a book bearing that overall title. I
found myself unexpectedly struck, even thrilled,
by the following paragraph:

> That man is the product of causes which had
> no prevision of the end they were achieving;
> that his origin, his growth, his hopes and fears,
> his loves and his beliefs, are but the outcome
> of accidental collocations of atoms; that no fire,
> no heroism, no intensity of thought and feeling,
> can preserve an individual life beyond the grave;
> that all the labors of the ages, all the devotion,
> all the inspiration, all the noonday brightness
> of human genius, are destined to extinction in

the vast death of the solar system, and that the whole temple of man's achievement must inevitably be buried beneath the debris of a universe in ruins—all these things, if not quite beyond dispute, are yet so nearly certain that no philosophy which rejects them can hope to stand. Only within the scaffolding of these truths, only on the firm foundation of unyielding despair, can the soul's habitation henceforth be safely built.[31]

The last sentence is the one that thrilled me most. Despair! Here was the habitation that my soul had been seeking! Throw that master switch, and feel the relief spread through your mind and body, feel the burden of hope lift from your shoulders, feel the freedom of no longer needing to make anything happen for anybody, including yourself. I copied the sentence down on a little slip of paper, and for fully fifteen years I carried it in my wallet as something like my secret mantra.

And in all candor, it worked for me. When I came across the book, I was exhausted and depressed in the wake of Richard M. Nixon's 1972 defeat of George McGovern, the candidate I had worked for tirelessly in the vain hope of ending the bloodbath of the Vietnam War. Ironically, given Russell's lifelong political activism, his gospel of despair calmed me down. It excused me from politics and all such larger efforts and returned me, with paradoxical energy, to the private adventure of young adult life. As the years passed, I didn't think about the quote every day, but it stayed there in my wallet, my firm foundation, my good luck charm.

And then I lost my wallet.

Actually, my wallet was stolen from a gymnasium locker. As I reassembled its contents (driver's license, my one credit card, etc.), I had to look up and copy out the Russell quote again. But this time, though I still responded to the rhetorical swell of the prose, I noticed that Russell had claimed only that the science on which he had laid his firm foundation of despair was "nearly certain"—I noticed that I had no independent knowledge of the scientific basis for his existential claims. And I reflected that in any case science itself must surely have moved on in important ways since his day. But then I noticed something else. I noticed that my Russell romance had not been my only such love affair. I had been rhetorically smitten at least twice before, and both times the words were very like Russell's.

Though I read French, I have read only a few entire books in that language. Among those few are two that affected me so strongly that I can recall where I was when I read them, most especially where I was when I read the entrancing sentences I will now quote, passages that I might have recalled (but did not) when I later read Russell.

The first comes from the existentialist philosopher Albert Camus in *The Myth of Sisyphus* (1942). Camus, like Russell, asserts that despair and—going beyond Russell—even suicide is the logical response to the human condition, but then he goes on to assert that we must rebel against that logic and embrace the absurdity of life and even of happiness. The embrace of hope and the refusal of suicide constitute the rock that the mythical Sisyphus, standing in for you and me, must endlessly push to the top of the mountain of existence, knowing that as he reaches the summit—as hope approaches realization and despair nears triumph—the rock will tumble punishingly to the bottom, forcing him to a new, absurd renewal of his embrace of life and hope. The famous concluding sentence of *Le mythe de Sisyphe* (I am scarcely alone in admiring it) is

Cet univers dèsormais sans maître ne lui paraît ni stérile, ni futile. Chacun des grains de cette pierre, chaque éclat minérale de cette montagne pleine de nuit, à lui seul, forme un monde. La lutte elle-même vers les sommets suffit à remplir un coeur d'homme. Il faut imaginer Sisyphe heureux.

To him this now Lord-less universe appears neither sterile nor futile. Every particle of that rock, every mineral glint from that mountain swathed in night, forms a world unto itself. The struggle toward the peaks is itself enough to fill a man's heart. One must imagine Sisyphus happy.[32]

The second quote that initially so transfixed me was from a French scientist who was a close personal friend of Albert Camus, as I learned only while writing this postscript. This was Jacques Monod, a molecular biologist and Nobel laureate, whose book *Chance and Necessity* (*Le hasard et la nécessité*, 1970) did not just assert that the universe was an accident but went on explain in impressive and, for me, almost mesmerizing detail how the accident might plausibly have happened. If Monod's account of the initial accident and of its inevitable continuation was correct, what did it say about the human condition? How were we to live? Monod answered that question as follows:

> *S'il accepte ce message dans son entière signification, il faut bien que l'homme enfin se réveille de son rêve millénaire pour découvrir sa totale solitude, son étrangeté radicale. Il sait maintenant que, comme un Tzigane, il est en marge de l'univers où il doit vivre. Univers sourd à sa musique, indifférent à ses espoirs comme à ses souffrances ou à ses crimes.*

> If he is to accept this message in its full meaning, man must finally awaken from his age-old dream to discover his total solitude, his radical strangeness. He knows now that, like a nomad, he stands at the margin of the universe where he must live. A universe deaf to his music, as indifferent to his hopes as to his sufferings—or to his crimes.[33]

We were to live as nomads, then, looking in from the outside upon a settled universe deaf to the most plaintive strains from our violins.

What to say? In my twenties, I was a sucker for such stuff, as you may already have noticed. Worse, I was painfully slow to notice my own posing. It took the passage of some time and the small, salutary shock of having my wallet stolen to induce me to triangulate these three professions of secular faith and then to realize, with an inner blush, that what I had wanted was simply closure, a way to stop thinking about questions whose answers were beyond my reach. Camus may have earned his existentialism in the French Resistance. Monod must have earned his both there and in his laboratory. I could not, I cannot, do other than honor their memory. But my own identification with them seemed a meretricious, adolescent borrowing. It seemed the secular equivalent of what the German theologian and martyr of the German Resistance Dietrich Bonhoeffer (1906–1945) had scorned as "cheap grace." I felt a little ashamed of myself.

Then, further years later, having begun for no reason that I could easily name to intermittently and anonymously attend services at an Episcopal church, I heard a hymn whose opening stanza jolted me awake by its use of some of Russell's language—specifically, his "*firm foundation* of unyielding despair":

How firm a foundation, ye saints of the Lord,
Is laid for your faith in his excellent word!
What more can he say than to you he hath said,
To you that for refuge to Jesus have fled?

Keeping the secular company I then generally kept and with the reading habits that I then had and still have, I was accustomed to hear or read that religion was a refuge for those not brave enough to face the uncertainties of the real world. That seemed to be an old and familiar charge, but I now asked: Had Russell, too, not sought a refuge, a "soul's habitation," and finally had he not claimed rather more firmness for it than was really there?

The thought came and quickly went, but it would come back. Eventually, I would start to wonder whether Camus and Monod were finally much different from Russell. Even granting that faith was "ridiculous" (the word I heard so often from my friends), was it any less ridiculous to pretend that one was wretched Sisyphus and then declare that by sheer force of imagination one was happy about it? Absurdity indeed! Why should this form of nonsense be regarded as any less ridiculous than religion, once the spell of eloquence was broken? But then, too, why belittle Camus for coping with his perceived dilemma as well as he could? And if we were all becalmed in the same boat—Camus, Monod, Miles, Russell, and the anonymous Anglican who wrote the hymn—what were we to do? Sink the boat? Was I now to be ashamed of all of us? What good did that do them or me, or anybody?

Finally, I began to inch past that shamefaced embarrassment. I began to wonder whether it was really wrong for any of us to seek some kind of interim closure, some way of coping with our own invincible ignorance. Over the years, I had been an avid reader of popular science, always fascinated by the latest findings but increasingly aware that each new discovery raised at least as many questions as it answered. The research conducted at the Large Hadron Collider of the European Organization for Nuclear Research (CERN, the Conseil Européen pour la Recherche Nucléaire), for example, baffles me as much as it does any other untrained reader, but I have followed its development over the past several years not just with interest but also with a little research question of my own. Suppose they demonstrate the existence of the Higgs boson, or "God particle," I asked myself. Suppose they confirm the Standard Model of modern particle physics. Will that not simply raise a host of new questions and open further wide vistas for research? And is that not the result of *every* new discovery?

Well, they did demonstrate the existence of the Higgs boson. Peter Higgs won his belated Nobel Prize. And, yes, the success of CERN has opened wide vistas for further research. One scarcely needed to be a physics genius to predict that it would. But apparently it has increased our ignorance rather more than I would have imagined or predicted. Steven Weinberg, a Nobel laureate in physics, concluded a 2013 article titled "Physics: What We Do and Don't Know" in the *New York Review of Books* with the following rather chastened sentences: "Physical science has historically progressed not only by finding precise explanations of natural phenomena, but also by discovering what sorts of things *can* be precisely explained. These may be fewer than we had thought."[34] If science is the pinnacle of human knowing and physics the pinnacle of science, and if science is crucially limited even for those gifted few—Weinberg's "we"—who know science best, where does that leave the rest of us? Confessions like Weinberg's are far from unknown among scientists: I have a small collection of them, addressing not provisional results within a science but the outer limits of science itself. I have begun to imagine human knowledge and ignorance as tracing a curve of asymptotic divergence, such that with every increase in knowledge, there occurs a greater increase in ignorance, the result being that our ignorance always exceeds our knowledge, and the gap between the two grows infinitely greater, not smaller, as infinite time passes.

Conscious ignorance was a great human breakthrough, perhaps the greatest of all, for until our remotest ancestors could tell the difference between ignorance and knowledge, how could they know they knew anything? They could have had no conscious control over their own incipient knowledge. When did the breakthrough to conscious ignorance occur? The actual date, the actual occasion, the actual individual who first gained conscious control of the difference between knowing and not knowing are all beyond historical recovery, but some such moment surely has to have come long before the invention of writing and therefore much earlier than the earliest text in *The Norton Anthology of World Religions.*

One thing Russell was right about, I do believe, is that Earth and the human species alike have finite life expectancies: "all the labors of the ages, all the devotion, all the inspiration, all the noonday brightness of human genius," as he wrote, "are destined to extinction in the vast death of the solar system, and . . . the whole temple of man's achievement must inevitably be buried beneath the debris of a universe in ruins." Just as an individual man may conclude that life is too short for him to answer the larger questions that loom around him—whose answers, for all he knows, may impinge quite directly on his most personal decisions—so it may be for the human species as a whole. You may die never having learned the one fact that would have changed everything for you. In just the same way, extinction may befall the human species as a whole with key questions still unanswered and perhaps even unasked.

Scientific progress is like mountain climbing: the higher you climb, the more you know, but the wider the vistas of ignorance that lie before you on all sides. You think you are approaching the summit, but then you see that you have merely reached a point from which you can see not just that the summit stands higher still but that your mountain is surrounded by other mountains, an entire range, and where does it end? Alexander Pope described this experience in a poem (*An Essay on Criticism*, 1711):

> So pleased at first the towering Alps we try,
> Mount o'er the vales, and seem to tread the sky,
> The eternal snows appear already past,
> And the first clouds and mountains seem the last;
> But, those attained, we tremble to survey
> The growing labors of the lengthened way,
> The increasing prospect tires our wand'ring eyes,
> Hills peep o'er hills, and Alps on Alps arise!

As the human species nears extinction, will science have been superseded by something that differs from it as much as it differs from philosophy or philosophy from religion? When we reflect on how slightly, on the one hand, our genome differs from that of the chimpanzee and how greatly, on the other hand, our knowledge surpasses that of our genetic cousin, can we not imagine that a further

minor genetic alteration might bring into existence a being whose knowledge might dwarf ours
as much as ours dwarfs that of the chimpanzee?

How can we know just how brutal or
wonderful—or, above all, how basic—the surprises that lie ahead may be? Kay Ryan, an Alexander Pope for our moment in history, captured
this distinctly contemporary kind of uncertainty
in a poem titled "On the Nature of Human
Understanding":

Say you hoped to
tame something
wild and stayed
calm and inched up
day by day. Or even
not tame it but
meet it halfway.
Things went along.
You made progress,
understanding
it would be a
lengthy process,
sensing changes in your hair and
nails. So it's

strange when it
attacks: you thought
you had a deal.[35]

So, do we have a deal or not? Those who speak
the language of "we *now* know" think they have a
deal, and more power to them, even if the civilization that pays their bills may have only another
fifteen years before sliding into a decline no technology can reverse.[36] For the rest of us, suffice it to
say then that if religion rests on human ignorance, it
rests on a firm foundation indeed, and the same may
be said if the claim is made that religion rests on a
foundation of fear. Of course it does, and how could
it not? The man or woman who first grasped the
difference between knowing and not knowing must
surely have been all but instantly aware that her or
his ignorance vastly exceeded his or her knowledge
and that he or she had every good reason to fear the
unknown. Though nowadays some of us are under-
standably impressed with what we collectively know
(which most often means being impressed with what
other people know and we believe), our ignorance
still exceeds our knowledge, and we still have emi-
nently good reason to fear the unknown.

And how do we cope with that? However we cope with our ignorance, we cannot, by definition, call the coping knowledge. What do we call it? Let's not give it a name, not even the name *religion*; but if we can concede that religion is conceivably *among* the ways that humankind has coped with the permanence and imponderability of human ignorance, then we may discover at least a new freedom to conduct not just a comparison of one religion with another but also an even broader comparison. If we grant that we must all somehow go beyond our knowledge in order to live our lives, then how do religious modes of doing just that compare with other modes, call them what you will? Since the challenge is practical rather than theoretical, the comparison should be of practices, of expedients, rather than of theories— yet the hope must be for a reasonable way of coping with the practical impossibility of our ever living a perfectly rational life.

Religion seems to me to bear one aspect when considered as a special claim of knowledge and quite another aspect when considered as a special acknowledgment of ignorance. One may certainly be struck by the peculiar way in which the claims of knowledge made in the course of religious revelation always seem to arrive coupled to the disconcerting claim that ordinary human knowing could not have reached what is about to be conveyed. But rather than construe this declaration as arrogant boasting, one may take it as confessional humility. Leszek Kolakowski, a disillusioned Polish Marxist who became a distinguished historian of ideas, wrote in an essay titled "The Revenge of the Sacred in Secular Culture" (1973):

> Religion is man's way of accepting life as an inevitable defeat. That it is not an inevitable defeat is a claim that cannot be defended in good faith. One can, of course, disperse one's life over the contingencies of every day, but even then it is only a ceaseless and desperate desire to live, and finally a regret that one has not lived. One can accept life, and accept it, at the same time, as a defeat only if one accepts that there is a sense beyond that which is inherent in human history—if, in other words, one accepts the order of the sacred.[37]

Inevitable defeat is the plight of Sisyphus; but while Camus takes acknowledging the failure of religion to be a condition for the acceptance of that defeat, Kolakowski sees religion as the acceptance itself. I myself do not accept that there *is* "a sense beyond that which is inherent in human history," only that there may be. How can we know, either way? And, just as important, how soon can we know? Kolakowski, no less than Camus and the others, returns me to the closure question.

Science is immortal, but you are not. History is immortal: planet Earth could have vaporized, and on some unimaginably distant planet on some unimaginably remote future date, another civilization could still choose to use the terrestrial year as a unit of time measurement. But where does that leave you? You have a life to live here and now. You're going to go with something. You're going to know that you have no perfect warrant for it. But you're going to go with it anyway.

Kidding yourself? Yes, I suppose so. The adult in you wants to reserve judgment until all the facts are in, however long that takes. The kid in you wants to declare the answer adequate and put the ball in play. In the laboratory, the adult wins. In real life, even for those who spend their professional lives in the laboratory, the game goes to the kid. Herbert Fingarette (b. 1921), an American philosopher admired for his work on the philosophical problem of self-deception, has written:

> It is the special fate of modern man that he has a "choice" of spiritual visions. The paradox is that although each requires complete commitment for complete validity, we can today generate a context in which we see that no one of them is the sole vision. Thus we must learn to be naive but undogmatic. That is, we must take the vision as it comes and trust ourselves to it, naively, as reality. Yet we must retain an openness to experience such that the dark shadows deep within one vision are the mute, stubborn messengers waiting to lead us to a new light and a new vision. . . . Home is always home for someone; but there is no Absolute Home in general.[38]

Life as lived is the challenge against which it makes most sense to assess the utility of religion, as indeed of much else; and in my judgment, life as lived is the context in which it makes most sense to explore even the more arcane and exotic contents of a capacious collection of texts like *The Norton Anthology of World Religions.*

Having thought for so long about the existential meaning of science in the stark and tragic terms of Russell, Camus, Monod, and Kolakowski, I confess that I experience a certain relief in thinking of play rather than explanation as quite plausibly the evolutionary taproot of religion. The idea is not a new one. I am drawn to it partly because investigation for the sheer fun of it has everything to do with pure science as well. Isaac Newton—still, I think, the greatest scientist of all time—wrote famously, and rather poignantly: "I do not know what I may appear to the world; but to myself I seem to have been only a boy playing on the seashore, and diverting myself in now and then finding a smoother pebble or a prettier shell than ordinary, while the great ocean of truth lay all undiscovered before me."[39] I find Newton's words poignant only because he certainly did not appear to the world as a boy playing on the seashore. Au contraire! But do we wrong science if we take its findings in the aggregate as Newton took his? This year a Higgs boson, next year an even smoother pebble, an even prettier shell, and so forth until extinction interrupts the beachcombing?

I think not. And I think of religion as a second boy playing with that first boy on the beach but saying to him at a certain point, "This has been fun, but it's getting dark, the tide is coming in, supper may be almost ready, and I'm going home. The ocean will still be there tomorrow. If you come along, I promise to tell you a story on the way."

NOTES

The intellectual debts incurred in the foregoing discussion are far greater than could be registered even in a far longer list of footnotes than appears here. The subject matter touched upon could obviously command a far longer exposition than even so lengthy an introduction as this one has allowed. I beg the indulgence alike of the students I may have overburdened and of the scholars I have failed to acknowledge. JM

1. Robert N. Bellah, *Religion in Human Evolution: From the Paleolithic to the Axial Age* (Cambridge, MA: Harvard University Press, 2011).
2. Anthony Appiah, *As If: Idealization and Ideals* (Cambridge, MA: Harvard University Press, 2017), p. 5 (emphasis Vaihinger's).
3. Ibid., p. 3 (emphasis Appiah's).
4. Anemona Hartocollis, "Bloomberg Gives $1.8 Billion to Johns Hopkins for Student Aid," *New York Times*, November 18, 2018.
5. Todd Boss, "It Is Enough to Enter," in *Pitch, Poems* (New York: W. W. Norton, 2010), p. 15.

6. Kevin Schilback, "Religions: Are There Any?" *Journal of the American Academy of Religion* 78.4 (December 2010): 1112–38.

7. Frans de Waal, *The Bonobo and the Atheist: In Search of Humanism among the Primates* (New York: W. W. Norton, 2013), p. 210.

8. Daniel L. Pals, *Eight Theories of Religion*, 2nd ed. (New York: Oxford University Press, 2006); Michael Stausberg, ed., *Contemporary Theories of Religion: A Critical Companion* (London: Routledge, 2009). Strikingly, they do not overlap on a single entry.

9. Feynman is quoted in Dennis Overbye, "Laws of Nature, Source Unknown," *New York Times*, December 18, 2007.

10. See p. 55 in *The Norton Anthology of World Religions, Volume One* (New York: W. W. Norton, 2015).

11. Clifford Geertz, "Religion as a Cultural System," in *The Interpretation of Cultures: Selected Essays* (New York: Basic Books, 1973), p. 90 (emphasis his).

12. Ibid., p. 125.

13. Ibid., pp. 193–233.

14. Tomoko Masuzawa, *The Invention of World Religions, Or, How European Universalism Was Preserved in the Language of Pluralism* (Chicago: University of Chicago Press, 2005).

15. All Bible quotations in this introduction are from *The Holy Bible, Revised Standard Version* (New York: Thomas Nelson & Sons, 1952).

16. Mark C. Taylor, *After God* (Chicago: University of Chicago Press, 2007). Whether this is what the martyred German theologian Dietrich Bonhoeffer had in mind when he dreamed of "religionless Christianity" in letters from the Nazi prison where he

would be hanged in 1945 is debatable. The phrase is highly suggestive, but, tragically, Bonhoeffer died before further developing his ideas.

17. On diffuse religiosity in its Eastern guise, see James Robson on "Daoism in Today's China and Beyond," in *The Norton Anthology of World Religions,* Volume One (New York: W. W. Norton, 2015), pp. 1492–1495.

18. Herbert Butterfield, *The Englishman and His History* (Cambridge, England: The University Press, 1944), p. 119.

19. Lynn Hunt, Margaret C. Jacob, and Wijnand Mijnhardt, *The Book That Changed Europe: Picart and Bernard's "Religious Ceremonies of the World"* (Cambridge, MA: Belknap Press of Harvard University Press, 2010), p. 2 (emphasis added).

20. Ibid., p. 5.

21. Ibid., pp. 155–57 (emphasis added).

22. Jean Frederic Bernard, quoted in ibid., p. 241 (emphasis in original).

23. See James Robson, "The Lasting Influence of 'Jesuit Daoism'" in *The Norton Anthology of World Religions,* Volume One (New York: W. W. Norton, 2015), pp. 1475–1477; and Nicholas Trigault (1577–1628), [A Seventeenth-Century Jesuit Missionary in China], *The Norton Anthology of World Religions,* Volume Two (New York: W. W. Norton, 2015), pp. 1138–1141.

24. Donald S. Lopez, Jr., *From Stone to Flesh: A Short History of the Buddha* (Chicago: University of Chicago Press, 2013).

25. *The Quest of the Historical Jesus* is the colorful title of the English translation first published in 1910; Schweitzer's sober German title was *Von Reimarus zu Wrede: Eine Geschichte der Leben-Jesu-Forschung*

(From Reimarus to Wrede: A History of Research into the Life of Jesus). Hermann Reimarus and William Wrede were earlier scholars.

26. See "THE SECOND VATICAN COUNCIL (1965), *Nostra Aetate*" in *The Norton Anthology of World Religions,* Volume Two (New York: W. W. Norton, 2015), pp. 1320–1323. For the background in World War II and its aftermath, see John Connelly, *From Enemy to Brother: The Revolution in Catholic Teaching on the Jews, 1933–1965* (Cambridge, MA: Harvard University Press, 2012).

27. James Frazer, *The Golden Bough: A Study in Magic and Religion: A New Abridgment from the Second and Third Editions* (Oxford, England: Oxford University Press, 2009). Frazer's extravaganza eventually grew to twelve volumes, now out of print. For a more recent and more richly informed account of the evolution of religion, see Robert M. Bellah, *Religion in Human Evolution: From the Paleolithic to the Axial Age* (Cambridge, MA: Belknap Press of Harvard University Press, 2011).

28. See Denise A. Spellberg, *Thomas Jefferson's Qur'an: Islam and the Founders* (New York: Knopf, 2013).

29. Marcel Proust, *In Search of Lost Time*, Volume Five, *The Captive; The Fugitive*, trans. C. K. Scott Moncrieff and Terence Kilmartin, rev. D. J. Enright (New York: Random House, 1993), 5:245–46.

30. See Preface, *The Norton Anthology of World Religions,* Volume One (New York: W. W. Norton, 2015), pp. xliv–xlv.

31. Bertrand Russell, "A Free Man's Worship," in *Why I Am Not a Christian, and Other Essays on Religion and Related Subjects*, ed. Paul Edwards (New York: Simon and Schuster, 1957), p. 107.

32. Albert Camus, *Le mythe de Sisyphe* (Paris: Éditions Gallimard, 1942), p. 168 (my translation).

33. Jacques Monod, *Le hasard et la nécessité: Essai sur la philosophie naturelle de la biologie* (Paris: Éditions du seuil, 1970), pp. 187–88 (my translation). On Monod's friendship with Camus, see Sean B. Carroll, *Brave Genius: A Scientist, a Philosopher, and Their Daring Adventures from the French Resistance to the Nobel Prize* (New York: Crown, 2013).

34. Steven Weinberg, "Physics: What We Do and Don't Know," *New York Review of Books*, November 7, 2013, p. 88. Cf. Dennis Overbye, "Finding Higgs Merely Opens More Puzzles," *New York Times*, November 5, 2013.

35. Kay Ryan, "On the Nature of Human Understanding," *New Yorker*, July 23, 2011, p. 30.

36. Justin Gillis, "U.N. Says Lag in Confronting Climate Woes Will Be Costly," *New York Times*, January 16, 2014: "Nations have so dragged their feet in battling climate change that the situation has grown critical . . . , according to a draft United Nations report. Another 15 years of failure to limit carbon emissions could make the problem virtually impossible to solve with current technologies, experts found."

37. Leszek Kolakowski, "The Revenge of the Sacred in Secular Culture," trans. Agnieszka Kolakowska, in *Modernity on Endless Trial* (Chicago: University of Chicago Press, 1990), p. 73.

38. Herbert Fingarette, *The Self in Transformation: Psychoanalysis, Philosophy, and the Life of the Spirit* (New York: Basic Books, 1963), pp. 236–37.

39. Isaac Newton, quoted in Sir David Brewster, *The Life of Sir Isaac Newton* (New York: J. and J. Harper, 1831), 300–301.

CREDITS

INDEX